HOW TO LICENSE YOUR MILLION DOLLAR IDEA

Everything You Need to Know to Make Money from Your New Product Idea

Harvey Reese

John Wiley & Sons, Inc.
New York • Chichester • Brisbane • Toronto • Singapore

*For my family, from whom never is
heard a discouraging word. For Thelma,
Andrea, Tory, Gerson, and Esther.*

In recognition of the importance of preserving what has been
written, it is a policy of John Wiley & Sons, Inc., to have
books of enduring value published in the United States
printed on acid-free paper, and we exert our best efforts
to that end.

Copyright © 1993 by Harvey Reese
Published by John Wiley & Sons, Inc.

Library of Congress Cataloging-in-Publication Data

Reese, Harvey.
    How to license your million dollar idea : everything you need to
know to make money from your new product idea / Harvey Reese.
        p. cm.
    Includes index.
    ISBN 0-471-58051-1 (cloth : acid-free paper). — ISBN
0-471-58050-3 (paper : acid-free paper)
    1. Patent laws and legislation—United States—Popular works.
2. Inventions—United States. I. Title.
KF3114.6.R44 1993
346.7304'86—dc20
[347.306486]   92-44310

Printed in the United States of America

10 9 8 7 6 5

ACKNOWLEDGMENTS

I asked for technical help and opinions from some of the finest patent attorneys in the city of Philadelphia, and each responded with enthusiasm, intelligence, and honesty. My heartfelt thanks, therefore, to Dann Dorfman, John Lezdey, Ronald Panitch, John McNulty, and Louis Weinstein. Also, I appreciate the help of the Mead Corporation in allowing me to reprint some of their material, and a special nod to Loren Taylor, of Playtime Products, for his permission to use some of his correspondence. My agent, Lyle Steele, who has seen them come and go, always made me feel that this book was special. For his attitude, enthusiasm, and helpful suggestions, I am most grateful. Finally, this book would never have happened without the advice, love, wise counsel, and unceasing support of my wife, Thelma.

CONTENTS

Success is just a matter of luck.
Ask any failure.

—*Earl Wilson*

The steps in creating and shaping up a simple idea, and how to turn it into a monthly royalty machine.

The six-step, can't-miss system for spotting an opportunity, and how to profit from it by creating the perfect product.

How to evaluate the merits of your idea, and how to protect it with or without patents, copyrights, or trademarks.

INTRODUCTION

Money can't buy happiness,
but it will get you a better
class of memories.
—Ronald Reagan

This is a test. What do the following phrases have in common?

It takes money to make money.

The bigger the risk, the bigger the profit.

Go for the burn. No pain, no gain.

The answer: They are all false. Physical therapists tell us that smart exercising needn't cause pain to be beneficial. And I can testify that you don't have to put your savings at risk to turn a handsome profit.

In 1933, during the Great Depression, Charles Darrow an out-of-work plumber of Allentown, Pennsylvania, found himself with plenty of time on his hands. Just to be doing something, he dreamed up a game about Atlantic City real estate and called it Monopoly. He licensed the rights to Parker Brothers, the big game company, and never had to work another day in his life. That was more than a half century ago, and the royalty checks are still coming in. His total investment was some time, ingenuity, and brain power. These are investment assets that we all possess. If you have the will to put them to use, this book will show you how to enjoy a return on your investment that may be beyond your wildest dreams.

One quick note: Although I've used the pronoun "he" throughout this book for the sake of easier reading, the material herein refers to both women and men, who, needless to say, share equally the potential for good ideas and the desire to get rich from them.

SOLID GOLD POUND PUPPIES

The business section of any bookstore is loaded with books that show you how to spend your money. You can become a Wall Street tycoon, you can invest in pork bellies, you can be a real estate mogul, or you can be a donut shop operator. You name it. Just ante up your money and take your best shot. Go for the burn. And getting burned may be exactly what will happen.

On the other hand, manufacturers pay billions of dollars each year in royalties and licensing fees to people who supply them with profitable ideas. Incredible fortunes are being made every day by ordinary people who have licensed their valuable ideas to willing buyers. A few years ago, a factory worker at a Ford plant near Cincinnati came up with a toy idea called "Pound Puppies," which started out as a gift he made for his wife. But he was smart enough to recognize its sales potential and smart enough to realize that he should turn it over to professionals, who know what they're doing. So he licensed his idea to the Tonka Company. They sold more than 50 million puppies, and the royalties turned Mike Bowling, the ex-factory worker, into a multimillionaire. Stories like this are commonplace. Ordinary people are reaching for and achieving the biggest jackpots of their lives through licensing. The nice thing is that you can do it too.

Almost everybody gets at least one Pound Puppy idea; the crime of the century is that so few people have the will to do anything about it. They mean to get around to it one day, but as even Sophocles knew, centuries ago, fortune is not on the side of the faint hearted.

THE HOW-TO-NOT-GO-INTO-BUSINESS-FOR-YOURSELF BOOK

The purpose of this book is to show you how to make your fortune without risking one. If you'll supply the will, I can supply the knowledge. And you can keep your money in the bank. I'm billing this as the How-to-Not-Go-into-Business-for-Yourself book. The trick is to have other people spend their money and take the risk. If you have an idea that can turn a profit, company presidents all over would love to hear from you, and it would be their pleasure to give you a cut of

Licensing Is an Equal Opportunity Activity

the proceeds. Any president would be delighted to give you $5.00 for every $100.00 in receipts you can create for his company. It's simply good business.

Licensing is an equal opportunity activity. Good ideas can come from anyone, with or without connections. If it can earn a profit, the manufacturer doesn't care if you're young or old, rich or poor, male or female, black or white. He doesn't care if the idea comes from Mother Theresa or Attila the Hun. If your idea is a money-maker, you will be welcome. A man named Percy Bridgeman once said, "There is no adequate defense, except stupidity, against the impact of a new idea." You can call successful businesspeople lots of names, but "stupid" usually isn't one of them.

TAKE THE MONEY AND RUN

You can earn big money fast through licensing because that's what it is all about. If your idea is really good and you put it in the right hands, there's no upper limit to your profit potential. And if you've licensed your idea to a successful, professional marketing company, you'll probably be getting royalty checks while the person who wants to do it himself is still looking for seed money. For some people, looking for enough capital to start a new business is a lifetime quest. And if they finally do collect the money, the statistical chance of success is very grim. The other way is to turn your idea over to professionals—people who know what they're doing—then take the money, and run. In the movie *Patton*, George C. Scott, who plays General Patton, explains to his troops that war isn't about dying for your country. It's about getting the other guy to die for *his* country. Well, licensing isn't about investing your money. It's about getting the other guy to invest his. Let him have the risk and the glory. You'll take the royalty checks.

Perhaps one day, one of your ideas will make you a millionaire. But in the meantime, you keep your job, you keep your cash, you keep your house, and you don't get nasty calls from creditors or your bank.

IS YOUR IDEA IN A COMA?

At one time or another, almost everyone has had a clever idea just "pop" into his head. It just stays there, without nourishment or attention, until it finally slips into a coma. Like Sleeping Beauty, this lovely idea just lies there, day after day, year after year, waiting for a Prince Charming to come along. Unfortunately, life's not a fairy tale and the Prince will never show up. What does happen is that eventually this person sees "his idea" on the market and hollers "Foul!" because someone beat him to it.

If you're not prepared to act on your ideas, someone is *always* going to beat you to it. That's what capitalism is all about. Benjamin Disraeli, the nineteenth-century British statesman, said, "Success is the child of audacity." Lots of people get the same idea. The one who does something about it gets the prize, and the others get to complain about having bad luck. Properly exploiting just one useful idea may change your life forever. It happens all the time. There's a system to help you do it effectively. It's called the CRASH Course and this book is going to carefully lead you through it. You won't be the same when you're finished.

CONVERTING YOUR BRAIN INTO AN IDEA FACTORY

Actually, as I'm sure you know, ideas really don't just "pop" into your head. And they don't come from divine inspiration. You're not going to awaken one morning and say "Hey Martha, I just dreamed up a terrific new accessory item for computer owners!" The idea that just seems to appear is

Ideas Don't Just Pop into Your Head

actually the end product of a defined step-by-step process. And once you understand what it is, you'll be able to develop ideas almost at will. The process is not automatic, you have to really work at it; but if you follow the prescribed steps, it won't let you down. I create and license new ideas for a living. It's all I do. I can't imagine a nicer occupation—getting paid for my own creativity gives me a rare and wonderful feeling.

THE OPPORTUNITY OF FAILURE

Years ago, I owned a manufacturing company. It was profitable but highly leveraged. I owed my bank almost $2 million. During the Carter presidency, as you may recall, interest rates shot up to an incredible 25 percent. I drained the company's assets trying to keep up with the interest payments until finally, like thousands of other companies, I was forced to go out of business. More than 100 people lost their jobs, and I lost everything I owned.

But adversity often leads to opportunity. Mary Pickford, the old-time movie star, once said that failure is not about falling down, it's about staying down. I had to pick myself up in mid-life with no money and no job. I took stock of my assets and realized that what I was best at was dreaming up new products. I could no longer afford to manufacture them, so I decided to turn them over to others for a modest share of the proceeds. I quickly realized that what started out as a desperate course of action was actually a perfect career move.

In my business career, I've met people who have the management skills to run complex, highly successful companies but who have the imagination of a carp. On the other hand, I have creativity to spare, but I had demonstrated to my financial despair that management ability is not one of my strong points. Management types need me and I need them. It's proved to be a perfect match. I sold my first product idea to the very first company I showed it to. I've never looked back, and I've never been happier. My only regret is the years I spent managing a factory. Many of the companies I originally licensed product ideas to have since gone out of business. But new companies come along all the time. They all need new products, and I'm still here to provide them.

WHAT I HAVE THAT YOU CAN HAVE (OR DO HAVE)

I'm not just being modest when I tell you that I'm not a genius—I'm an ordinary guy—and the product ideas I create are not scientific breakthroughs. What they are are simple, commercially sensible concepts that a manufacturer can examine and visualize selling profitably. I do have two attributes, however, that separate me from many other people, and that have enabled me to earn more money than would have been likely from any other endeavor.

1. I have the confidence that I'll never run out of ideas because I've developed a system for continually producing new ones. It always works, and at any given time I have more ideas than I can handle.

2. I have the confidence that, if my idea is sound, I can always get money for it. I have a battle-scarred, time-tested, technique for doing it, and I seldom miss. There's a system for effectively preparing your idea, getting an appointment to show it to the right people, and saying the right things when you get there. That's the CRASH Course, and that's what this book is all about.

There's no mystery to creating and licensing commercially sensible ideas. There are just two easily mastered systems involved: one for developing ideas and the other for getting them licensed. I intend to teach both of them to you in this book because there's more than enough room out there for all of us. Whatever I know, you'll know. And if you apply it, there's no telling how much money you can make.

Research shows that we all possess creative traits. Artists and geniuses don't have a monopoly on creativity, and although you may not be able to compose a sonata, you can be creative in other ways. A simple, workable, idea, properly exploited, is also the product of creativity. Thomas Alva Edison, America's most prolific inventor, always remembered that his ideas had to be practical. He often said that he didn't want to waste his time inventing anything that wouldn't sell. You may not reach his level of genius, but once you get into the swing of it, you'll see that creating commercially viable ideas is really not that difficult. Abraham Lincoln thought up one (a patent for an inflatable system to help boats navigate shoals); Dorothy Lamour thought up one (a patent for a torpedo guidance system); even six-year-old Bobby Patch thought up one (a patent for a toy truck). Just about anyone can do it. The hard part is having the courage and drive to turn it into profit. The chief executive officer of Martin

Marietta Company, Norman Augustine, once commented that "Motivation will almost always beat mere talent."

YOU CAN'T MAKE A SCORE IF YOU DON'T HAVE A GOAL

There are many fine books in print to help you think big, act big, and dress big. But then what? Sure, having a winning attitude is important, but if you don't have a goal to apply it to, what have you accomplished? What good are two highly motivated, all-pro football teams, if the field they're playing on doesn't have goal lines? This book offers you a very specific goal to strive for; it shows you exactly how to get there; and, I hope, it will motivate you to get started. If I can help you gain some of that think-big confidence, and if I can persuade you to focus it on the goal of creating and licensing commercial ideas, then there's no limit to how far you can go.

You Can't Make a Score If You Don't Have a Goal

LOSERS NEED NOT APPLY

I have books on my desk that tell the stories of inventors, scientists, and researchers who have earned millions of dollars in royalties for their inventions. Certainly these people deserve the credit and riches they've received, but they're not the audience I had in mind when I thought about this book. My original thought was to include some of their stories as positive examples, but I've since changed my mind. It would serve no purpose to explain how Willard Bennett invented the radio frequency mass spectrometer, or how Frederick Cottrell invented the electrostatic precipitator, or how Gordon Gould invented optically pumped laser amplifiers. I want, instead, to provide profitable information to the person who, in idle moments, may not develop an idea worth many millions, but who, quite conceivably, might develop and license commercial ideas worth $100,000, or $500,000, or maybe even the magic $1,000,000. It happens all the time; probably much more often than you think. Charles Schwab once noted that a person could succeed at anything for which he has unlimited enthusiasm.

If you could meet some of the people I know who have made fortunes for themselves with simple ideas, you'd understand why I say that anyone with reasonable intelligence can do it. Nothing terrible will happen if you fail. Something wonderful may happen if you succeed. The only real losers are those who won't even try. As the baseball pundits say, "You can't steal second if you won't take your foot off first."

I don't want to create the impression that licensing commercial ideas is a simple sure-fire way to make money, because it's not. But what business is? The difference is that participants in licensing prefer to invest instead in their God-given creativity and turn the financial risk over to others. They make the smartest investment of all, in themselves.

While it's true that almost all of us dream up ideas that have value, it's shocking how few of us do anything about it. To some extent, it's because of a lack of knowledge, but to a larger extent it's due to a lack of confidence. Mary Kay Ash, the founder of the hugely successful Mary Kay Cosmetic Company, summed it up well when she said, "If you think you can, you can. And if you think you can't, you're right." Whatever your idea is worth—$10,000, $100,000, or $1,000,000—success is within your reach, and the results may forever improve your quality of life and the well-being of your family. Winners can see an opportunity in every problem. Losers tend to see problems in every opportunity. If you're not already a winner, the information in this book can make you one. If I didn't believe that, I wouldn't have written it.

FREE AT LAST!

It doesn't matter how much or how little money you have or how far you went in school; if you're a prisoner of a work-for-wages-job or have no job at all, this book can set you free. Fortunes are made from exploiting useful ideas. Perhaps it's time for you to make yours. After all, America is still the land where dreams come true.

Free at Last!

1

THE CRASH COURSE FOR SUCCESSFUL LICENSING

*Ten thousand great ideas
filled his mind;
but with the clouds they fled
and left no trace behind.*

—Thompson

The first real job I ever had was with an advertising agency. One day I had occasion to ride with the president in his car to visit a client. It was many years ago, but I can still remember the ride quite clearly. My boss had a steel bar, about 18 inches long, somehow welded onto the car's steering column. It extended out past the steering wheel on the right-hand side, and at the end was a little rectangular metal plate with a clip on top. This held a memo pad and a pencil on a string. It looked like what it was, a Rube Goldberg invention, and I shudder to think what it did to the car's resale value. But that didn't seem to matter to my boss.

He explained that whenever he bought a new car, the first thing he did was take it into a sheet metal shop to have a contraption like this installed. Since he was in the business of selling ideas, he reasoned that whatever notion popped into his head was a potential company asset. Any idea not captured on paper is an idea waiting to get lost. Ideas are money and nobody wants to lose money. He understood that until he wrote down the idea, his mind was its prisoner. The mind repeats the idea over and over, for fear of forgetting it, and in the meantime all new thoughts are blocked out. It just takes a moment with a pencil and paper to get it back to work.

I've developed this same kind of fanaticism. I trust nothing to memory and immediately write down whatever business thought pops into my head. Random thoughts become lists, lists become outlines, and outlines become plans of action. Outlines give structure to what you do. They unclutter your head and keep your mind on track. They let your brain know you mean business. It's much like an airline pilot's safety check. He may have performed this function hundreds, or even thousands of times, but it's too important to do without a written list. There can't be shortcuts. It could mean his life as well as the lives of all his passengers.

I go to a local gym several times each week to use the exercise equipment. I use the same machines in the same order, at the same settings, each time I go. The gym, however, knows the weaknesses of its customers. Every time I go, I receive my personal checklist. After I use each machine, I'm expected to enter the date and check an appropriate block. I'm not finished with my workout until all the blocks are checked. Even here there are no shortcuts. Keeping that checklist up to date keeps me on track in my fitness program, just as other checklists keep me on track in my business.

This book can serve as your own checklist if you do every step and don't look for shortcuts. These systems work and can serve as your guide and mentor. The CRASH program is designed to bring you a degree of wealth and with it, I hope, an enriched life and the pride that comes from creating something of value for others.

ALL ABOUT THE CRASH PROGRAM AND WHY IT WORKS

There's a passage in *Alice In Wonderland* where Alice comes to a fork in the road and doesn't know what to do. She asks the Cheshire Cat which road to take, and the Cat, logically, asks Alice where she wants to go. "I don't much care where," Alice answers. "Then," says the Cat, "it doesn't matter which way you walk."

You may be reading this book because you, too, are at a fork in the road. Unlike Alice, however, you'll know where you're going, and the CRASH Course is going to be your road map. I think you'll like what's waiting for you at the end of your journey.

Gimme a "C"!

The "C" in the CRASH Course stands for *Create*. Nothing can happen until you create the idea. It's the seed from which can grow a bountiful harvest. There's a simple, proven procedure for sparking ideas that works for me and for just about every other creative person I know or have read about. I'm confident it will work for you as well. And even if you already have plenty of good ideas, I think you'll still find the suggestions in Chapter 2 interesting. Nobody has ever suffered from too many good ideas.

Gimme an "R"!

The "R" in the CRASH Course stands for *Research*. Is it really a good idea? Is it original? Can it be done? Will it sell? Assuming you come up with the right answers to these questions, you need to know how you can protect your idea in a safe, prudent practical manner.

I spend a great deal of time in the book on this step. Whenever I lecture, the questions I'm most frequently asked center on the protection of an idea. I've met people who are so frozen with fear that someone is going to steal their ideas that they do absolutely nothing with them. Patent attorneys tell me they get calls from inventors who inquire about fees, but won't reveal their ideas, even in the most general terms. One day, these inventors will be carried off to the old folks home with their precious ideas still locked within them. Did they have ideas worth millions? Could they have lived out their lives in splendor? We'll never know and neither will they. But their ideas are safe.

In Chapter 3, I will show you simple, inexpensive ways to protect your concept, often without the need for an attorney. But if you do need one, I'll show you how to keep fees at a minimum. Nobody hates to pay legal fees more than I do, and it's surprising how much you can accomplish on your own.

Gimme an "A"!

The "A" in the CRASH Course stands for *Action.* You have the idea. It's innovative and it's protected. Now's the time to show it to the world. This step, discussed in Chapter 4, deals with the preparation of your presentation, the selection of prospects, and the tricks to get a face-to-face appointment with the decision makers. There are professional and effective ways to do these things, and I'll explain them to you.

Gimme an "S"!

The "S" stands for *Show 'n Tell.* This is make-or-break time. It's when you go out and sell your ideas to prospective licensees. In Chapter 5, we'll discuss what to show them and what to tell them. I'll give you tips on how to make presentations and prep you on what questions to expect and how to answer them. This is also the right time to discuss the potential use of agents. Do you need them? How do you find them? How do you negotiate with them?

Gimme an "H"!

If the creation of an idea is a seed, the other steps in this program are designed to care for and nurture it until maturity. Now it's time to reap the *Harvest*. And that's the "H" in CRASH. Exactly how bountiful the harvest will be, and in what form and under what circumstances must be spelled out in a contract. This is the payoff time, and Chapter 6 will help you get everything you're entitled to.

A sample of the contract I use myself is included. If you follow it, you probably won't need an attorney. And if you do use attorney, you'll be a better client for understanding the process. I'll point out what provisions must be included for your protection, what provisions are negotiable (and how far), and what provisions you must never agree to. You will have worked hard to get to this stage, so you don't want to blow it with an unsatisfactory agreement. Follow this chapter carefully and that won't happen.

Y-E-A-H . . . CRASH!

I can't think of a better way of summing up the CRASH Course than by quoting the first-century Roman philosopher, Epictetus:

No great thing is created suddenly, anymore than a bunch of grapes or a fig. If you tell me you desire a fig, I must first answer that there must be time. Let it first blossom, then bear fruit, then ripen.

What was observed almost 2,000 years ago is no less true today. The CRASH Course is designed to guide you every step of the way from seed to harvest. And now we start. It's planting time. I hope your crop is bountiful.

By the way, someone who knew how to nurture the seed of creativity must have seen my old boss's car because there's now a terrific product on the market that's a big improvement on his old welded steel bar. I'm sure you've seen it. It's a notepad clipped to a plastic base that fastens to the dashboard by a suction cup. Nearly every stationery store and auto accessory store sells them. I wonder if my old boss complains that someone stole his million-dollar idea. It was staring him in the face, all those years, and he never realized it. If he had taken his idea and licensed it, he would probably have made more money than he ever did with his advertising agency.

2

CREATING THE IDEA

How to Identify
a Market Need and
Create the Solution

I don't care a damn for the invention.
The dimes are what I'm after.
—Isaac M. Singer
(Referring to his sewing machine)

There is a widely held misconception that creativity flourishes best in an unstructured environment. However, interviews with creative people show that their environments and work habits tend to be quite regimented. This self-imposed discipline allows them to get the work done. People who rely on the creation of original ideas as a profession have long understood that it is not a haphazard activity. Otherwise, how could they stay in business? The work structure functions like the banks of a river. Without them, the river meanders all over until it simply disappears. Creative thought requires similar boundaries. Without them, it too meanders all over and finally disappears.

A clearly defined system is at work in the creative process, even if the participants follow it subconsciously. Once you recognize what's going on, and break it down into steps, you can condition your brain to produce ideas almost at will. There are only six steps involved, and they are certainly not complicated.

Libraries are filled with books of theories about the creative process. The subject has fascinated investigators for centuries, and in many respects it's still a mystery. The consensus, however, is that while few of us are geniuses, virtually all of us have far more creative ability than we could possibly imagine. Apparently, no direct correlation exists between an exceptionally high IQ and creativity, which has more to do with your mind-set and the amount of discipline you bring to the task. If you look for ways to be creative—if you really work at it in a systematic way—the results may astonish you.

As a memory device to explain my creative process, I took the first letter of the action word in each step and put them together. They spell ICICLE. You would think I was terribly clever if I could get them to spell something like MONIES or CREATE, but unfortunately they don't. All they spell is icicle.

To follow Reese's ICICLE System for creating commercial, profitable ideas you must:

I. *Identify Your General Goal or Objective.* Define the general problem.

C. *Concentrate on Developing a Solution.* Do research.

I. *Identify Your Goal Again.* This time pinpoint it.

C. *Concentrate Again.* This time focus on the narrowly defined goal.

L. *Let It Go.* Go to sleep; go to a party. Let your subconscious go to work.

E. *Eureka!* When you least expect it, the idea just "pops" into your head.

I realize this sounds too simple to be true, but if you'll give ICICLE a chance, you'll be astonished at how creative you can be. Most great ideas are characterized by their simplicity, and an idea about creativity itself needn't be an exception. If you read through the books on the psychology of creativity, you'll see that, while researchers remain perplexed about *why* thoughts and ideas are created, they've long understood the process. With slight variations, this is the classic evolution of a process that hasn't changed since the beginning of time. Psychologists perhaps have more learned ways of describing it, but when you ignore the left brain–right brain stuff, it's still just Reese's ICICLE System.

So forget the movies. Forget about knocking a beaker over in a laboratory, accidentally mixing up two chemicals, and thereby unlocking the secret of the atom. If you want solid, commercial ideas, you have to work at it. Let's look at the system step by step.

STEP 1. IDENTIFY YOUR GENERAL GOAL OR OBJECTIVE

The creative process begins the moment you pick up a pencil and commit a general goal or objective to paper. A daydream ends, a plan of action begins. Just as you can't get your troops to march if you don't give them marching orders, so you can't get your brain into production until you've told it what to produce. Or, as Seneca said many centuries ago, "When a man does not know what harbor he is making for, no wind is the right wind." Defining a goal, or selecting a harbor, sets your

Creativity Starts When You Reach for a Pencil

imagination on an exciting voyage with a crisp wind filling its sails.

Watch Out for Falling Fruit

Sometimes, defining a goal or objective is as simple as bumping into it. Say you're a dentist and in the normal course of your work you wished a certain kind of tool existed that would make one of your procedures easier. This is opportunity knocking, yet 10,000 dentists won't hear it over the noise of their drills. If you have the mind-set to be creative, and if you're viewing your world with profit opportunities in mind, you'll recognize one when you see it. As an old Chinese saying goes, "When heaven drops a date, open your mouth." Just think. If you had been that dentist, and if you created and licensed the tool to a dental equipment manufacturer, how many thousands of other dentists would say "Hey, I had that idea years ago!"

However, heaven isn't dropping any fruit on most of us. We have to pick our own. And the way to start is to look for a goal or objective. This is the most difficult (and most critical) part of the process because a clear definition of the problem often suggests the solution. The trick is to recognize it. If, about 10 years ago, I had said, "Do you notice the tough time people have carrying their luggage through airports?" it wouldn't have taken you long to create those collapsible little carts that are sold by the millions. Anyone of us could do it, but the one who got rich was the person who had the imagination to recognize the problem. Jacques Lipchitz, the famous artist, once defined creative imagination as the ability to invent the wheel while observing a man walking.

Plunging Ahead

In the *New York Times*, of June 3, 1992 on page 17 of the third section, I noticed this headline:

TOILET PLUNGER IS THE MODEL
FOR DEVICE TO RESTART HEARTS

How can you resist reading a story like this? Here's the first paragraph:

> A mother and son in San Francisco, who used a toilet plunger to revive a man whose heart had stopped, have inspired development of a simple new suction device that some experts say works better than traditional cardiopulmonary resuscitation.

The article proceeds to tell how the new device works and that it could help save some of the more than 500,000 Americans who die of heart problems outside a hospital each year. The boy who saved his father with the toilet plunger (he did it twice over several years) suggested to doctors that they have one by the bed of every cardiac patient. The article says that most of the doctors simply found this to be an amusing suggestion and went about their business. Opportunity was knocking, but the physicians weren't home to callers.

Three doctors did take the suggestion seriously, however, and after some design work and testing, the Cardio-Pump was born. Patents have been applied for and a manufacturer has been licensed to manufacture and distribute the product worldwide. If it works as well as it is supposed to, you can assume the doctors who hold the patent will never have to lift another tongue depressor for the rest of their lives. And do you suppose the other doctors are still amused?

Being Part of the Solution

Problems like this are all around us, just waiting to be solved. Even so obvious a concept as a left shoe and a right shoe was only conceived a little more than 100 years ago. Most of us are not part of any problem, and we're not part of any solution. We're just sort of standing around not paying much attention to either. But if you can get yourself to become part of the solution, you have a good chance of becoming well off—and you may even become rich.

The starting point is to develop the belief that you can do it . . . and that you *deserve* the rewards of your accomplishment. Losers are not only convinced that they can't do it, they think it's part of some grand universal plan that they should be where they are in life. It's as if, to them, their personal success would spoil some cosmic system. And then who knows what would happen? It's the *que sera, sera* syndrome. Winners even do better in hospitals. Studies have shown that people who fight for their recovery by calling the nurse all the time, demanding to see the doctor, always asking for medicine, and in general just being a demanding patient, have a much better survival rate than those who lie in their bed quietly and say, "Whatever will be, will be."

Turning Irritations into Opportunities

To uncover a goal or objective, the logical place to start is with what you know: home, hobbies, work. Just as pearls come from irritated oysters, product ideas often come from common, daily irritations. Is there some chore at home you hate to do? Would some kind of new product make it easier? Whatever irritates you is most likely irritating millions of others as well. The person who first came up with the idea of a little frame to hold a leaf bag open was undoubtedly irritated when raking the lawn. I bought one of these gadgets a few years ago and bless the inventor every time I rake my leaves. It's hardly a breathtaking product and shouldn't even be mentioned in the same breath as the Cardio-Pump, but it answers a need and provides a profit. What more is necessary?

Climbing the Corporate Ladder

Many new ideas are work related for obvious reasons. You see a problem or bottleneck on the job and your creative mind starts to think of a solution. To avoid problems later, and perhaps to get the rewards you're entitled to, it's a good idea to find out your company's policy on new product development. If you're entitled to be compensated, you should know it up front.

Proper ownership of an idea is easily recognizable at both ends. It's the middle ground that can get murky. If, say, you're a computer program operator with a medical company and, on your own time, you develop a new type of fishing rod, this is clearly none of your employer's business. At the other extreme, if you're a scientist working in the company's laboratories, and you develop an exciting new chemical process, this obviously belongs to the company. But suppose you work in the shipping department and, borrowing some of the laboratory's materials, you work at home on your own time and develop a new method for coating pills. Who does this belong to?

The idea for Band-Aids was developed by a then-low-level employee at Johnson & Johnson, and he automatically turned it over to the company. Is it any wonder that he retired years later as a senior vice president? Also, the scientist who developed the Post-It Notes is a 3M employee, and the product obviously reverted to them. Both companies, I'm sure, have clear policies for rewarding employees in such situations. If your company is small and doesn't have a well-defined policy, I don't think it's out of line to ask that you be given a memo of understanding before you submit any ideas to them. Once they already have your idea, it's a little too late.

When Is an Idea Not an Idea?

I've come to realize that when most people complain about "their idea" being marketed by someone else, they never actually had an idea to begin with. What they really had was an idea *for* an idea. They didn't actually sit down and work out the design for a product to hold a plastic leaf bag open. They didn't apply for a patent, they didn't make a sample, they didn't do any research, they didn't develop a marketing plan. All they did, a few leaf raking seasons ago, is say, "Dammit! Somebody oughta come up with a contraption to keep these damn bags open!"

Well, their wish was eventually granted and somebody did. Nevertheless, when the "contraption" finally did appear on the market, thousands grumbled that they had the idea first. They didn't have an idea. They had a thought. You can't license a thought, but you can get rich from an idea. As someone named Mona Crane once observed, "Opportunity is sometimes hard to recognize, if all you're looking for is a lucky break."

Get It in Writing or Kiss It Goodbye

Magazines are another rich area to mine for ideas. I get about a dozen magazines every month and pore over the ads quite carefully trying to think of new features for products that would give me an edge over the competition. Another approach is to watch the people around you: at work, in the malls, on the streets. See what they do, listen to what they say, observe how they're dressed. I do a lot of mall watching and have developed some very good ideas in this fashion. In the immortal words of Yogi Berra, "You can observe a lot, just by watching." Whatever you do, always carry a notebook and write down any random thoughts that come into your head.

Here are some bits and pieces from one of my own little notebooks. Although the jottings wouldn't make sense to anyone but me (as you can tell from the way they're entered), my only purpose was to capture my thought of the moment. Every few weeks, I review my little notebook, enter the thoughts that still seem interesting (and that I can still understand) into my permanent idea book, and discard the others.

My permanent idea book contains several years' worth of observations, thoughts, and rough doodles. When I review it, I'm able to see a variety of new product ideas beginning to take shape. I try to prioritize these ideas, and turn my energies toward developing what seem to be the most promising. At the same time, as I discard passé ideas, I am entering new ones. It's an ongoing process, and my inventory of new ideas is always larger than I can develop and sell.

You Do It Because You Do It

It's my discipline that I never go anywhere without a note-book and pencil in my pocket. They're on my dresser, next to my wallet, and automatically go into my pocket each morning along with my wallet and my money. Musing over a new product idea is never far from my thoughts, and if I think of something, I can't rest until I've captured it on paper. It's what I have to do, and I just do it. I never doubt that I'll come up with my next new product. Not ever.

I sometimes wonder how great cartoonists like Schultz or Larson can come up with such funny cartoons every day, week in and week out. My guess is that, like me, they're never without a notebook and pencil, and thinking about new cartoon ideas is never far from their minds. It's what they have to do, and they just do it. I'm sure they never doubt that they'll come up with their next cartoons. Not ever.

If you tell yourself that it's what you have to do, you'll do it too. Belief releases the creative juices, so never doubt that you can do it. You can. I know you can. Just make a start and the rest will follow.

Send a Fax to Your Brain

Your brain registers untold thousands of sights, events, and impressions every day. There's not a waking moment when some occurrence isn't being absorbed. It's a deluge, and your poor brain is so busy just taking notice that it sometimes has difficulty separating the important from the humdrum. That's where note taking comes in. It's the way to tell your brain, "Hey, this is really important, so file it somewhere that's easy to reach." Don't try to evaluate your thought on the spot. Write it down, worry about it later. Afterward, when you've had time to reflect, you can review your notes and separate the valuable from the valueless. Before you know it, by periodically reviewing your notes, a course of action will become clear and you'll be on your way. So buy a notebook. It's the best 49-cent investment you'll ever make.

Finding Your Niche

I happen to create many toy products, so one of my methods for establishing goals is to wander through toy stores looking

---

Playtime.
A Subsidiary of Tyco Toys, Inc.

Harvey Reese Associates

Att: Mr. Harvey Reese

Re: 1993 Product

Dear Mr. Reese:

Thank you for coming to visit us at Toy Fair. As you witnessed first hand, good things are happening at Playtime. We have many new product categories and fresh new products throughout our line <u>including seventy individual products from outside inventors/designers</u>. How many companies can claim a number like that?

In 1993 we will be adding to all areas of our existing business and will be <u>expanding into new categories like sports and outdoor products</u>. <u>We are looking for innovative new additions</u> to our existing lines and new lines or categories of products to expand our business.

Attached is a Playtime and a Helm catalog for your reference. We're counting on you to show or send us more exciting products this year!

I look forward to seeing or hearing from you soon.

Best Regards,

PLAYTIME PRODUCTS, INC.

Loren Taylor
Executive Vice President

LT/js

Enc.

for niches and gaps to fill. This is what corporations do all the time. They're constantly examining their industry, trying to find areas that are not fully developed. They call it "niche marketing," and I figure my job is to beat them to it. I try to put myself into the shoes of a toy manufacturer and determine what someone in that business would like to produce. I almost always come home from the stores with ideas and rough thoughts. Also, once you've established yourself as a professional, many companies will solicit your ideas and guide you into areas they want to develop. For instance, on page 28 there is a letter I recently received along with a catalog from one of the leading toy companies.

Playtime Products is a division of Tyco Toys and is one of the most respected names in the industry. Not only do they state with pride that 70 of their current products are from outside sources, but they indicate the new areas targeted for development. This same letter went to their entire list of freelance product developers and it's one way an enlightened company keeps ahead of competition.

To proceed with our program, let's assume that your hobby is camping, that there are several camping manufacturers in your area, and that you've decided to look for a new product for that industry. This is all you require for the first step. You have your general goal. You've sounded reveille for your brain.

STEP 2.   CONCENTRATE ON DEVELOPING A SOLUTION

In Step 1, you identified a simply stated goal or problem to solve; to create a new product for the camping industry. In Step 2, you must concentrate on the camping industry and find out everything you can about it. You're looking for a niche, and that requires putting the industry under a microscope. Go to libraries, go to stores, talk to people, read magazines, write down everything you see and learn. Fritz Maytag, president of Anchor Hocking, writing in the *Harvard Business Review*, said, "If you're going to make rubber trees, you better go to Malaysia and see the damn rubber trees!"

By concentrating on the camping industry, you'll be looking to uncover the specific need for a new product or important ways to improve existing products. In Step 1, you sounded reveille for your brain. Here, in Step Two, you prepared to give it its marching orders. You're seeking a target of opportunity and when you've found it, it's time to move to Step 3.

STEP 3.   IDENTIFY YOUR GOAL AGAIN

Your originally stated goal needn't be anything more than a rambling, loosely stated direction in which to proceed: "I want to do something in the camping field" is good enough. If you live in Baltimore, Maryland, for instance, and you want to drive to your friend's house at 123 Maple Street in Denver, Colorado, your general goal is simply to head west and find your way to Denver. When you arrive there, you focus on your narrower goal of finding 123 Maple Street.

For the sake of discussion, let's say your research uncovered a need for a new type of disposable, biodegradable eating utensils. That's the niche you were looking for, and you're now able to instruct your brain, with precision, where you want it to concentrate. You restate your goal in a precise way by saying to yourself, "Forget about blankets, tents, boots, and cots, my objective is to develop a completely new line of *biodegradable eating utensils that can be reused or disposed of,* whichever the camper wishes." You have a 10-word objective, so it's time to move on.

If Step 1 was your brain's reveille, and if in Step 2 you gave out marching orders, Step 3 is where your brain smartly starts its march toward its destination.

STEP 4.   CONCENTRATE AGAIN

When sportswriters talk about a star athlete, they usually say something like, "He has great hands and terrific concentration," or maybe, "She has all the natural skills and terrific concentration," or often, "He has enormous speed and terrific concentration." Can we detect a pattern here? Having this unique ability to give 100 percent of their attention to what they're doing seems to be the one trait that all great athletes have in common. And that's what's required of you here. Not casual concentration, *intense* concentration.

Now that you have a precisely defined goal, you have to bring all your focus to bear on it. You should be thinking about camping utensils day and night—making drawings, trying experiments, making prototypes, filling page after page with sketches and doodles, doing research, reviewing your material over and over again—and all the time thinking, thinking, thinking.

Just as you spend quality time with your children, so you have to spend quality time with your idea. And quality time here means concentrated time. No radio, no television, no telephone. Just you and the problem, eyeball to eyeball.

How to Find a Fresh Idea

The creative process at its most primary level means thinking about a problem. It stays on your mind and invades your soul. The solution is so very close, but it disappears in a puff when you look in its direction. Tons of books describe methods to help you think creatively. They advocate techniques such as creative environments, quiet spaces, calmness, free association, and inner freedom. They tell you to do everything from solving children's puzzles to sitting in a tub or standing on your head. They show you special ways to sit and secret ways to breathe and mysterious ways to roll your eyes. All in the name of creativity. However, although sometimes the methodology may be laughable, the objectives are quite serious.

In a few simple words, all the juvenile puzzles and body-stretching techniques represent efforts to get you to think about a problem in an open, untethered manner. Certainly I support that objective. If you're constricted in your thinking by convention, it will stand to reason that your thinking is going to be conventional.

I know a great many creative people, and no two of them work on their creativity in exactly the same manner. If you do it best by standing on your head, who am I to complain? What every creative person is trying to achieve is a deep level of concentration. How you accomplish it is up to you. Three famous authors being interviewed about their work habits will show very little similarity in their answers. One may tell you that she writes longhand in her kitchen from 12 midnight until 5 A.M. Another will say that he has a computer in his den that he works on every day for as long as it takes him to write seven pages. The third writer may reveal that she dictates to a secretary every morning while still in bed. They didn't get these techniques from a book and they'd probably never suggest that budding writers follow these work habits. They merely found what works best for them, as I'm sure you'll find what works best for you.

Making Boredom Pay Off

If you belong to a health club, and if you ever exercise on a treadmill, then I know you'll agree it's the longest, dullest 30 minutes you can ever spend. My club understands this, so it locates most of the treadmills up front where there are lots of TV sets, lots of mirrors, and lots of comings and goings by the members.

In the back corner of the gym, a few more treadmills are in operation—no television programs; no distractions; relative peace and quiet. These are the machines I use, and I find it to be the most creative half hour of my day. There's no place to go and nothing to do, so my mind can gnaw on a problem like a bull terrier with a bone. I'm not alone. Men and women on either side of me are lost in their own problem solving. None of us got this out of a book on how to be creative, it's just something we independently discovered. Thinking time is where you find it. Surveys show that many people get their best ideas while showering or on the toilet. So keep a notebook handy. You never know.

Learning from Leonardo

Treadmills and toilets aside, over the long haul, what works best for me and for most other people is simple doodling. Nothing surpasses it for locking your attention onto the problem. A pencil is the best concentration device that's ever been created and, with one form of writing tool or another, it's how people have solved problems for many centuries. In his diaries, Leonardo Da Vinci, perhaps the most creative man in history, noted that his ideas came while doodling (he called it scribbling). What was good enough for Leonardo certainly should be good enough for the rest of us.

All research into the fascinating study of creativity indicates that results come not so much because of the creative technique itself, but from the level of intensity applied to a problem. Someone once asked a famous scientist what made him so special. He said it was because he could think about a problem for 15 minutes straight and other people can't. It sounds simple, but it's not. Try it sometime. A person who can focus on a problem that intently *is* special! But even if you can't match that performance, it's important to give it your very best shot.

The Assumption of Success

The other key factor in the creative process is what I call "the assumption of success." By assuming you'll find the solution, you significantly improve your chances of doing so. This is where Dale Carnegie's power of positive thinking comes into play. While I can't explain why it works, developing a winning attitude has helped thousands. We can only become what we first behold in our imagination.

Athletic coaches, regardless of the sport, all teach the assumption of success. If you're a golfer lining up a putt, you visualize the ball's route from the putter to the hole. If you're kicking a point after touchdown, you visualize the ball going through the uprights. You're seeing in advance the success of your endeavor—you simply can't succeed in sports unless you're able to do that. Calling it a winning attitude is not quite accurate. It's a winning *assumption.* No successful major league batter ever steps up to the plate without expecting to get a hit. Life's endeavors work the same way. Picture your

It's Time to Give Your Brain a Rest

creative work to be successful, and your brain won't let you down. It really works.

People who create—designers, writers, inventors—all expect to be successful in whatever they happen to be working on at the moment. An author doesn't start writing a book without expecting it to be a good one, and an inventor doesn't embark on a project without expecting to bring it to a satisfactory conclusion. If they didn't have this assumption of success, they'd have to look for different careers.

So if you've concentrated on the problem for as long and as hard as you can, and if you've developed the winning assumption about the outcome, and if you're brain-weary from the effort, it's time to give it a rest.

STEP 5.   LET IT GO

It's now time to slam your notebook shut and go to the movies, go to bed, or go to a party. Forget about the problem and give your brain a break. This is the incubation period. Your brain, now on automatic pilot, has an incredible capacity to sort through all the bits and scraps of information you've acquired about the problem. Scientists have long recognized this phenomenon, and yet how it works remains a mystery. That it does work, however, is undeniable. Your subconscious sorts it over, mulls it over, and thinks it over, and when you least expect it, the most wondrous thing happens. . .

STEP 6.   EUREKA!

You know what it's like when you can't remember someone's name? It's on the tip of your tongue, but you can't get it out no matter what you do. You think and think as hard as you can, but it just won't come. Later, seemingly out of the blue, while perhaps you're teaching limericks to your parrot, you suddenly snap your fingers and say, "Herman Smedley!" All of a sudden, you can remember everything you ever knew about dear old Smedley, down to the mole on the back of his neck.

The information was always there, of course, inside your brain. Your subconscious merely took its own good time to process it and bring it forward. That's exactly how good commercial ideas often are formed. Have a clearly defined goal, store the appropriate information, and give your brain the time to process it. Either the idea will pop out fully formed or, more frequently, a clue will emerge to put you on the right path. Either way, you're off and running.

PROVING IT WORKS

Unfortunately, as you've probably already guessed, Reese's ICICLE Process is not without its flaws. You sometimes have to repeat steps; it will only solve problems that are within the brain's capabilities; and, most important, it takes its own sweet time in doing it. The process may take seconds, days, weeks, maybe even years. And there's an element of luck and happenstance involved that can't be controlled. And yet it works.

I can remember a recent event when luck was on my side and I was able to go from a dead stop to identifying the problem, creating the solution, and actually selling the new product concept, all in one day.

An Umbrella for a Fish

I was wandering through a toy store, looking for some direction, when it occurred to me that I should focus on developing a new summer toy (*identify your goal*). I reasoned that since there are fewer toys available during that time of year, a toy manufacturer would welcome something to balance against the Christmas season. I wandered over to the display of summer toys (*do research*). What quickly became obvious was that the best summer toys all involved water. I was now able to narrow down my objective (*identify your goal again*) to creating a new toy that would involve water. I reached this stage in well under 15 minutes.

I thought hard about the problem (*concentrate again on the narrow goal*) while driving to keep a luncheon date, then gave my brain a rest (*let it go*) as I met my luncheon companion. Later, while driving home, the germ of an idea began to form (*Eureka!*), and I couldn't wait to put it on paper to see how it could work. In short order, I had the bugs worked out and faxed the concept off to a company with whom I do quite a bit of business. Within an hour I received a telephone call advising that everyone at the company loved the idea and that we had a deal and I should send them a contract. Rather than describe the item, the fax I sent is on page 38.

It's not rocket science, but if all goes well, lots of kids will be happy, lots of shopkeepers will be happy, the manufacturer will be happy, his employees will be happy, and I'll be happy. I'll grant you, this product is about as useful as an umbrella for a fish, but what has rocket science done for us lately?

I'm often asked if I'm fearful that someday I'll run out of ideas. I reply honestly that I'm not. As simple as it appears to be, the ICICLE System works for me, just as it has for others since the first time a human made a conscious effort to be creative. A system doesn't have to be complex to be valuable. As long as I can identify a problem, and as long as I do my homework, I'm confident the system will provide the solution.

Einstein was once asked his system for getting good ideas. "Actually," he replied, "I've only had one good idea, and

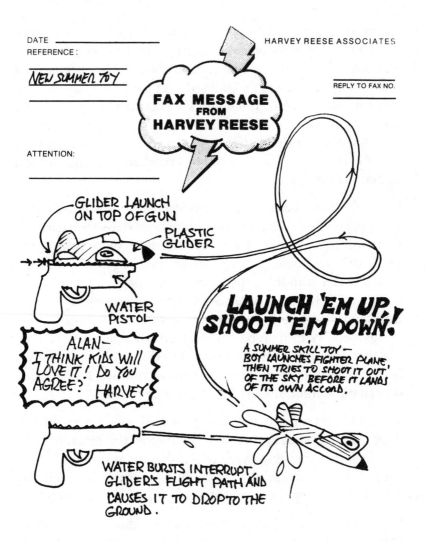

that's just a theory." Perhaps one good idea is all you'll need. If you exploit it properly, it may change and enrich your life. E. L. Simpson remarked, "Getting an idea should be like sitting on a pin. It should make you jump up and do something." In the next chapter, I'll discuss what that "something" should be.

3

RESEARCH

Evaluate the Originality and Market Need of Your Product, and Determine the Need for a Patent, Copyright, or Trademark

The harder you work,
the luckier you get.

—Gary Player

N ow that you have a commercially viable idea, it's time to research and protect it. In this chapter, we'll discuss the novelty of your idea and whether it merits the expense of a patent application. Then, we'll talk about how to go about obtaining a patent.

The U.S. Department of Commerce publishes an informative booklet called *General Information Concerning Patents*, which you can buy for two dollars. Refer to the Appendix for ordering information. According to the booklet, "Any person who invents or discovers any new and useful process, machine, manufacture or composition of matter, or any new and useful improvement thereof, may obtain a patent." This is called a utility patent, and obtaining one is a complicated, expensive process, usually requiring the services of a competent patent attorney.

STICK WITH THE McGUFFIN PRINCIPLE AND YOU WON'T GO WRONG

Although a utility patent is the best kind to get, many extremely profitable ideas either don't qualify for a utility patent or don't warrant the expense. That doesn't make these ideas any less valuable. You can probably still get ample, appropriate protection at a modest cost. There are design patents, trademarks, copyrights, and a whole host of other ways to protect your idea. And even if your idea doesn't qualify for any of the traditional methods of legal protection, it can still be quite valuable. Alfred Hitchcock used to say that it didn't matter if the hero in his movies was looking for a military code, stolen jewelry, or a secret formula. He called that object the *McGuffin*, and its only purpose was to move the action along. The adventure itself (with a happy ending) was the real story.

In our movie, the quest for profit is the real story, and a new product idea is just the McGuffin. People aren't interested in your invention as such, or your merchandising idea, or your book, or your play. They're interested in how it can be used to create profit. Any new and original idea that can create profit by its use has value and can be licensed. It's a McGuffin. Whether it's patented or not may be immaterial. Here's an example:

> A few years back, when soap operas were at the height of their popularity, it seemed as if everyone in the country was watching *General Hospital*. College kids were cutting classes, and people were actually staying home from work to watch "important" episodes.
>
> Thelma Reese, a college professor, and some friends, spent a riotous lunch one day trying to connect the relationships

between the various characters: who was married to whom; who was divorced from whom; who was secretly sleeping with whose wife or husband; who were really brother and sister but didn't know it; who were the real fathers of which kids; who was switched at birth with another baby in the hospital; who was really a murderer; who had amnesia and was not really the person he thought he was; who was plotting murder; and who was plotting the secret overthrow of the government. And that's not the half of it.

For the others it was just a funny lunchtime exercise, but for Thelma it was the germ of an idea. A few weeks later, after fully developing the idea, Thelma met with executives from ABC Television in New York and convinced them to give her the right to publish a full-color poster to be called "The Official History of *General Hospital*." It would be part history, part storyline, and totally funny. She then made a deal with a poster company that agreed to give her 40 cents for each poster sold. The company sold 110,000 copies, and Thelma became the Dr. Joyce Brothers of the soap opera world. Lecture agents wanted to put her on tour. The editor of a soap opera magazine called to discuss the possibility of a monthly column. Although she turned down most of the overtures, it was a glorious 15 minutes of fame.

This story illustrates that you don't have to be an inventor with a patented product or a secret formula to earn royalties. Thelma couldn't go to the Patent Office with the idea to make a history of a soap opera, but she made it a fully developed concept by securing the exclusive permission from ABC Television. And then she went out and found a company that saw money-making potential in Thelma's McGuffin.

Thelma earned $43,000 in royalties. She also earned some free trips to Hollywood, appearances on network and local TV shows, and guest appearances around the country on radio talk shows. She was the subject of many newspaper articles and was offered the possibility of a lecture tour (which she turned down), and the possibility of a monthly column (which she also turned down).

The royalty money, not a princely sum to begin with, went fast. Fame, as they say, is fleeting. What did remain was a new sense of pride and self confidence that has enabled her subsequently to achieve more professionally than she ever dreamed possible, including recognition in the form of invitations to White House luncheons. New ideas fly off her like sparks off a pinwheel, and some have turned out to be quite significant.

This true story highlights several facts:

1. The absence of a patent is not the death knell for a product idea. Often, it simply doesn't matter.

2. You can't merely have an idea for an idea. You have to spend the time to create a fully developed program. The more you leave for the licensee to do, the less valuable your idea becomes. If Thelma had gone to the poster company and asked for royalty money simply because she had the notion that a *General Hospital* poster would sell, she wouldn't have gotten to first base. Instead, she offered the idea, the ABC exclusive, research about the sales potential, a demographic profile, plus a fully developed sketch showing what the poster would look like. What she did, in effect, was make them an offer they couldn't refuse.

3. Finally, this story illustrates that *any* commercially viable product can be licensed if you find the right buyer. The "new product idea" I keep referring to needn't be a three-dimensional item that you can hold in your hand. Thelma's "product" was simply a turnkey scheme to make money. Let your imagination be guided by the profit, not the patent. Always remember that you're not in the invention business, you're in the McGuffin business.

Larry Holmes, the great boxer, sums up the concept much better than I ever could:

Why do you think I'm fighting? The glory? The agony of defeat? You show me a man who ain't fighting for money, I'll show you a fool.

You can almost substitute "inventing" for "fighting" and have this quote framed for your wall.

IS YOUR IDEA REALLY ORIGINAL? SO HOW COME NOBODY THOUGHT OF IT BEFORE?

Probably a dozen people, or maybe a hundred people, have thought of your exact idea before you did. That's beside the point. What's important is that none of them ever did anything about it. If you do something about it, then it becomes your idea to keep. If *you* don't, then you're just part of the mob. I make money on some of the most trivial, obvious ideas you can imagine. It's incredible that nobody did anything about them before; it defies logic. And yet, of all the presentations I've made over the years, in only one instance had the company previously thought of the identical idea. And even then, I sold the idea to one of the firm's competitors. And I'm still receiving royalty checks for it.

Don't Reinvent the Wheel—Someone Else Has Already Reinvented It

One reason I'm unconcerned about someone else having the same idea is that I thoroughly research it before spending my time and money. If a similar product presently exists because someone already has acted on the idea, or if it's an old idea that existed before, this is the time to find out. Your research may be as simple as visiting a few stores, talking to a few people, or checking through some books. Do whatever is required to assure yourself that a product incorporating your idea would truly be new and novel. It would be foolish to try to reinvent the wheel.

As a practical matter, if you've gotten this far in the process, chances are good that your idea is an original one. Don't be concerned if it seems simple and obvious. The more obvious the better! I'm almost embarrassed to tell you about some of the really foolish ideas I've sold.

My First New Product Idea

When my manufacturing business failed, and I decided to earn my living by developing and licensing new products, my first target was a small giftware company located near my house. The reason for this decision was simply that I was driving a junker car and was afraid to travel too far with it. And getting on an airplane to see a distant manufacturer was out of the question.

This company imported and distributed artificial flowers, so I obviously had to develop something in that category. What I finally came up with was a single silk rose attached to a greeting card and packed in an open gift box with a clear plastic lid. The cards, as I recall, said things like "A Rose for My Sweetheart."

I called the company, got through to the president, and made an appointment. I can still recall parking at the far end of the lot so no one would see the car I was driving. As nervous as I was, I must have made a decent presentation because the president loved the idea. We made up a simple agreement on the spot and I floated out of his office with a $4,000 advance check in my pocket. In short, I was paid thousands of dollars for taking an artificial rose, sticking it on a greeting card, and putting it into the bottom half of a hankie box. And the president actually thanked me for giving it to him!

It's hard to imagine a simpler idea, but the roses actually sold quite well, and I earned royalties from the product for several years. Not exactly a million-dollar idea, but enough to convince me that licensing was a legal way to coin money. What I learned was that by presenting a product properly, it is possible to sell almost anything. The president didn't say the idea was too stupid to be believed. He recognized that the company could make a profit from it and was happy to pay me my small share. That kind of insight is what makes a businessperson successful.

As in Life, Timing Is Everything

Don't be put off if your idea seems too simple. And, if somebody says, "How come nobody thought of this before?" that should be music to your ears. The trick is *not* to develop something that's years ahead of its time. A big payoff results from creating something that's about *15 minutes* ahead of its time. And you'll really hit the jackpot if you come up with something that's about *5 minutes* ahead. Like a surfer looking for the perfect wave, if you time it just right, you may be in for an exciting ride.

As you know, for fad items, timing is everything. "I have the next Pet Rock!" people tell me, with visions of moneybags dancing in their heads. They're chasing yesterday's dream product in a world that has passed it by. Times change, people change, tastes change. A fad product that was perfect three years ago would perhaps be a flop if it were introduced today. The Pet Rock was a lucky fluke that comes along every once in a while. Maybe you'll be the lucky person to come up with the next one. It's not likely, but it's possible.

How a Filthy Mouth Opened Purse Strings

A few years ago, a friend of mine, Budd Goldman, created and marketed a product called "The Final Word." It was about the size of an electric shaver, and pushing a button activated an electronic voice that pronounced vulgar epithets through a built-in speaker. The worst, most crude swearing you can think of is what came out of this little box when the user pushed the button. Classy, huh?

"The Final Word" was about as ludicrous as any product I've ever seen. And I've seen a lot of absurd products. If I had been asked to invest money in it, I would have told Budd to take a hike. But he was too smart to ask for my money or my advice. The product was a blockbuster of a hit; perfect for its time and perfect for its place. A little sooner or a little later, and it may never have gotten off the ground. Budd has a high-wire marketing company. He has more flops than hits, but the hits are usually big enough to more than make up for the failures. Nobody with a new product idea is ever turned away from his door without an audience.

"Widgets! Widgets! Get Me More Widgets!"

Most of the companies who will potentially license your product idea already have creative staffs who presumably do nothing all day but dream up new products. You might think that they're looking for the next hula hoop, but actually they're probably creating new versions of the products the company already manufactures. These are called "line extensions," and they are just what the name implies. If the company produces a line of 30 types of widgets, the research department is working on ways to extend the line to 40 widgets. New widgets, improved widgets, but always widgets. For instance, the headline of a recent Compaq Computer Company ad said:

> At Most Computer Companies, R & D
> Means Replicate and Duplicate

So when you come along with something really new, which can actually be sold right next to the widgets, the company thinks you're terrific. And you may scratch your head and wonder why this big company never thought of your obvious idea.

At the other extreme, small companies like my friend Budd's don't have research departments at all. And they're so busy with the day-to-day running of their business that they have almost no time to think about new products. So if you present yourself as a source for profitable new ideas, you'll be welcomed with open arms.

Surprisingly, nearly all the new products, for companies both large and small, arise from customers' suggestions. Most firms are simply not structured to encourage creative thinking. They respond rather than originate. That's why people like me are successful. And perhaps also people like you. Despite the huge research and development departments of many Fortune 500 companies, and despite the millions they spend in the search for new products, the majority of patents awarded every year go to small, independent inventors. These people—dreamers, innovators, and creators— are the superstars of the business world. Even when a large company does introduce an innovative product, it can almost always be traced back to one freethinker in the company who refused to be denied. Corporate committees are geared to funnel profits effectively, not to invent the products that earn those profits.

"Hey! They Stole My Idea!"

The insatiable demand for new products never abates. Thousands of new products are introduced every year, while thousands of others die quiet deaths. The cycle is as dependable as the tides. The supply never comes close to satisfying the demand, and yet the profession of dreaming up new products must be one of the least crowded in the country. There are probably 3,000 lawyers for every new product developer. Take that thought to bed with you tonight.

I urge you, therefore, not to worry about your idea having to be new and unthought of. It isn't new, and it was thought of dozens, or hundreds, of times before. What matters is that you're the one who's doing something about it. When your version appears on the market, all those other people will go around telling anybody who will listen, "Hey, they stole my idea! I had it years ago!" Whatever your idea is, it's going to be new to some company, and if it's good, the management will happily pay you for it. And they'll continue to pay you for it, perhaps for years and years, as long as it continues to produce profits. It may not be a million dollars, but maybe it'll be a second paycheck.

The End of the Free Ride

We're approaching the hard part of the CRASH program. You've worked diligently to develop your idea. It's your marvelous brainchild. Now you have to look at it coldly and dispassionately, as if you were a stranger. If it's not made of the right stuff, or if you're hesitant to spend the time or money to see it through, this is the go/no go juncture. You have to make two honest appraisals: Is there true commercial value to your product? Are you willing to do what it takes to get it licensed? If you're not enthusiastic about either, this is the moment to bring the effort to a halt. No penalty, no foul. Just go back to the drawing board, confident that your next idea will be twice as good as the one you have now.

The more intelligent research you do at this juncture, the easier it will be ultimately to license your new product idea.

Not Every Product Idea Has Commercial Merit

If your new concept was a toy, for instance, and if you could produce a few samples to let kids play with, certainly a prospective licensee would be interested in the results. If you took the samples to a day-care center and the kids really had fun playing with them, you would have a powerful sales point. On the other hand, if the kids showed no interest, or were quickly bored, the idea may need additional work or perhaps should even be abandoned. Regardless of the results of your research, you'll be better off for having the information. This is the time to get it, before you reach for your checkbook.

There are a few basic criteria in determining the prospects for your idea, but the most important thing I can tell you is to be honest with yourself. The majority of new patents are awarded to private individuals, and an estimated 90 percent of them are never commercialized. The obvious conclusion is that many millions of dollars are wasted every year in paying for patents on product ideas that simply have no commercial value. Nobody is going to be willing to tell you your idea has no merit. Your lawyer won't, your accountant won't, the model maker won't, and certainly your friends and relatives won't. Why should they? It's something that you have to find out for yourself. And you must not delude yourself about it. If you have the money to waste, a patent makes an attractive wall hanging, but it's an expensive piece of decor.

"Don't Confuse Me with Facts"

In the adult school course I occasionally teach on new product development, the semester always starts with the students absolutely refusing to reveal anything about their new product ideas. Each person thinks the rest of us have been put into the classroom by the devil to steal his or her idea. By midterm, however, they loosen up and there's no stopping them.

One older student showed me his drawings for a new concept in portable display fixtures that he intended to patent and offer for license to manufacturers of trade show displays. I happen to know something about that industry and quickly saw that what he had developed was inferior to displays already on the market. Existing displays are lighter, easier to assemble, and more flexible than what my student had come up with. It's not that his idea was bad, it's just that it was behind the times. He did have a unique locking system for his display, but it was not necessarily an improvement over existing generic devices. Only different.

Gently, I tried to point all of this out to my student, but he still bristled at my comments. So I backed off. It was none of my business anyway. Since he so frostily ignored my evaluation of his idea, here are two scenarios, one of which surely happened when the term was over.

Scenario 1: The Bad News.   In this version, my student takes his idea to a patent attorney. The lawyer either knows the idea has no commercial merit or he doesn't. Either way, he keeps his mouth shut. It's not his business to give commercial opinions. Patents are his business, and he informs the student that he can probably get a decent utility patent on the locking device. The student tells him to go ahead, and 18 months pass while the student waits with eager anticipation for the patent's arrival. The attorney proves to be correct, and finally he has the patent in hand. The student now sends form letters out to about a dozen manufacturers and naturally gets turned down every time (many don't even answer). The episode is finished, and he's out somewhere between $3,000 and $5,000. Meanwhile, he's angry at the stupidity of the exhibit manufacturers, who wouldn't know a good product if they fell over it.

Scenario 2: The Really Bad News.   Instead of going to an attorney, the student goes to an invention marketing company, that persuades him to buy a "market research" report on the potential for his idea. Shortly thereafter (surprise,

surprise), he receives an enthusiastic report about the thousands of trade shows held every year, and about the zillions of exhibitors who need booth displays, and about how brilliant he is to have created such an exciting new product for this enormous market. The student comes down from the clouds just long enough to buy everything the invention marketing company is selling except a new suit for him to wear when he accepts his award at the genius banquet. As with the attorney, the marketing company, even if it knows, will not tell the student his idea is worthless (except to the marketing company). So it costs him about $15,000 this time, and he still thinks the manufacturers are stupid.

The pity is that with some honest research, the student could have easily determined that his idea was not commercially viable. Unfortunately, even if he did find out, chances are he would have simply ignored the findings. His mind was set. Facts were irrelevant. After all, my student is no different from thousands of other inventors. It's no accident that so few patented ideas ever become commercial products. They don't deserve to be.

I've seen top-flight executives, who should know better, spend thousands of dollars to research their own idea's potential, only to ignore the negative findings. When personal egos are involved, it's very hard to be objective, regardless of who you are. But just as you fell in love for the first time, you have to be prepared to fall out as well. This is the moment to ask difficult questions, and to heed painful answers.

IS YOUR PRODUCT MARKETABLE?

1. *Is There a Real Need for the Product?* Are the benefits of your product obvious and desirable? Are the improvements over existing products easily apparent to potential customers, or must they be educated and sold on your product's advantages?

2. *Is There a Real Desire for the Product?* Can it be produced to sell at the right price? What will it take to get the consumer to buy it? How large is the potential market? Is the potential big enough to interest a prospective manufacturer? How quickly can your idea be copied by competitors? Is that an important consideration?

3. *Is the Manufacturer's Profit Likely to Be Sufficient to Warrant the Investment?* Assuming you have determined the right selling price to reach the maximum number of customers, and assuming you've researched and established the cost to produce the product, does that allow sufficient profit for tooling and normal marketing and distribution costs? Do you know the normal markup conventions of the industry in which your product will be sold?

There are obviously many other measures you can apply, and many other questions you must ask, depending on your concept. Will it work? Is it safe? Is it a fad? Is there much competition? Will it have adverse environmental impact? I've seen new product checklists that go on for several pages, but a checklist can only take you so far. More importantly, you must use your own good judgment and instinct. Just make sure you're giving yourself honest answers to legitimate questions.

If you've analyzed your idea as objectively as possible, and if you still like what you see, the other question is whether you're willing to do what it takes to get it licensed. It's not a free ride, but if you're willing to pay the fare, I think you'll enjoy arriving at the destination. So, if your research and good sense tell you it's an original, doable, profitable idea; and if you're committed to seeing it through, then it's time to move forward with the program. As Sophocles, the Greek playwright, said in the fifth century B.C., "Fortune is not on the side of the fainthearted." The idea you've come up with may be the best idea, most exciting idea, you'll ever have, and you only need one. Go for it!

IF THE IDEA IS SO GOOD, SHOULD I SPEND MONEY TO PROTECT IT?

Inventors in the true sense of the word, who have invented or discovered something truly profound, must, of course, seek patent protection. A strong utility patent can provide some piece of mind and serve as an excellent asset when licensing an idea. More on this later.

On the other hand, if what you've created can best be described as merely a clever, commercial idea, then it may neither merit nor need that kind of protection. The awarding of a patent has no direct bearing on the value of a product idea. If it warrants a patent, good sense says you should get one. But if it doesn't warrant one, that doesn't mean it's any less worthwhile. 3M's Post-It Notes aren't patented. Wouldn't you like to be receiving royalties on those little guys? Most of my own ideas are in the Post-It Notes' category (although not in their league), and my visits to a patent attorney's office are few and far between.

You Don't Have to Patent Everything That Moves

About five years ago, I created a funny little product called "Sip 'N Lips." Did you ever buy wax lips when you were a child? They're usually sold around Halloween and come as big, red lips for girls and silly looking fangs for boys. My new product concept was to make lips like these out of durable plastic instead of wax, and to have a funny loop 'd loop plastic straw attached. The idea was to make it fun for kids to drink their milk or other beverages. It was a quick product to dream up, and an easy one to license. It's still being sold, and I still receive royalties. It's quite popular, and I imagine it will remain on the market for years to come.

My point is that applying for a patent never occurred to the manufacturer or to me, although we probably would have been successful. By silent agreement, we decided the product did not warrant the expense and effort. More important, we also silently agreed that it would not be worth the financial outlay to defend the patent against any potential competitors. In other words, I never offered to patent the product. And it was never even a consideration for the manufacturer. These are business decisions based on experience and the understanding of what a patent can and cannot do for you. For some products, it's worth it. For other products, it isn't. This particular product has continued to prosper without legal protection, as the manufacturer and I were confident it would.

"Wanna Patent? Just Pay the Cashier"

Typically, the first thing a person does after creating a product idea is see a patent attorney. It's not the attorney's job to tell you if your idea has commercial merit, or if the attainment of a patent is even going to do you any good. You want a patent? The attorney will get you a patent. Pay the cashier on your way out. I urge you instead to pause, take a few steps back, and examine your idea in a critical light. A patent will cost at least several thousand dollars. If it's necessary, do it. Just don't do it automatically.

I could get a patent of one kind or another on virtually every product I've ever created, but I seldom do it. My product ideas usually don't warrant it. Somtimes, the licensee will get a patent in my name, which I then sign over to the company. I'll review this later when we look at a typical licensing agreement. For now, however, I want to stress that not having a patent shouldn't deter you from presenting your idea to companies. It's extremely unlikely that they're going to steal it. It's not because you're dealing with such righteous people, it's because it simply doesn't make good business sense.

WHY COMPANIES WON'T STEAL YOUR IDEA

1. *You'll Sue.* If they steal your idea, they know you'll sue and probably win. You'll have legitimate proof on your side regarding the idea's ownership. Even if you don't have a utility patent, or a design patent, you may have a trademark, a copyright, a nondisclosure registration number, or detailed, witnessed notes. You'll have something. They'll have to manufacture proof, perhaps requiring the cooperation of some employees, and that is risky business.

2. *You'll Take It to a Competitor.* If they were going to steal your idea, they'd have to do it when you made your initial presentation by telling you it was an idea they already had thought of. Logically, you would then take the idea to their competitor. So what will they have gained?

3. *You Can Be Bought Cheap.* The per-piece royalty they have to pay you is quite small, usually 5 percent, and that cost is passed on to their customers. It's factored in as part of the manufacturing cost, so it's cheaper (and safer) to pay you than to steal from you.

4. *You'll Cut Them Off.* The most important reason of all is that if they attempt to steal your idea you'll never bring them another one. And your next idea may be sensational!

Regardless of what you may see in the movies, companies aren't built by stealing ideas from starving inventors working alone in dingy basement laboratories. They may try to negotiate to pay us less than we want, but they're satisfied to pay us something. That's just good business. It's difficult for me to get people to believe this, but you're never going to achieve success at licensing unless you do. You can't simply stand guard over your ideas, and you can't try to patent every little concept you think of. Only your lawyer will thank you for that.

The Case of the Stolen Formula

Companies Aren't Lurking to Steal Your Idea

As previously mentioned, I sometimes teach a course at a local college on the subject of this book. The class is always overenrolled because, apparently, everyone is walking around with a secret million dollar idea. But it's difficult for me to cover all the course material because the students won't let me leave the subject of legal protection. These people are frozen with fear that some evil company president is waiting to steal their dream product. So their million-dollar idea remains safe, in their pocket, where it's undoubtedly been for years. If it's any good, someone else will eventually license it, and the procrastinators will tell everyone how they had the idea years ago. This is the Stolen Formula syndrome, and it's a very expensive malady.

Another emotion is involved, and this is as good a time as any to discuss it. In my classes, it's not uncommon to encounter people who actually have patents on their products and *still* won't go out and sell them. I've come to realize that the invention and the patent represent a dream. If the invention is rejected, the dream is rejected as well. By risking nothing, they gain nothing; but in their minds, they've also lost nothing. I've met unsuccessful inventors who are still showing off their inventions, years after there was any hope of ever licensing them. The drawings are yellow with age, but the dreams are still intact.

Sad to say, although many people profess to want success, they're really more comfortable with failure. Some years back, I saw a research paper on people's attitudes about work and was stunned to see how few workers wanted their boss's job and the responsibility that goes with it. I used to think that everybody wanted to be more successful. Now I've come to accept that most people simply want to be left alone.

But for those few of you who truly want more for yourself and your family, don't be deterred just because you think some big, bad company is out to steal your idea. They're simply not predisposed to do that. This fear would be the same as not leaving your house for fear that you'll be mugged. Yes, it can happen, but you can't allow fear to dictate your life.

Having said that, it would be naive not to acknowledge that there are still some unscrupulous operators out there who will try to steal from you just because that's what they do. Common sense dictates, therefore, that you should give your idea an appropriate amount of legal protection. The following section discusses the options that are available.

WHAT YOU SHOULD KNOW ABOUT PATENTS, COPYRIGHTS, AND TRADEMARKS

You may already have a general idea of the distinction between the basic forms of legal protection, but before we proceed, let's briefly review them.

1. *Utility Patents.* This is applicable for the invention or creation of a basic new process, machine, manufacture, or composition of matter. The idea must be primary, useful, original, and operational. Utility patents are designed to provide 17 years of exclusive use of an idea.

What they actually do is give the owner the right to sue others who may decide to bypass the patent.

2. *Plant Patent.* Here's how a government booklet describes this type of patent:

    The law provides for the granting of a patent to anyone who has invented or discovered and asexually reproduced any distinct and new variety of plant, including cultured spores, mutants, hybrids, and newly found seedlings, other than a tuber propogated plant or a plant found in an uncultured state.

    The Patent and Trademark Office (PTO), which is part of the Department of Commerce, will usually require that this type of application, unlike other patent applications, be accompanied by an exhibit. If a patent is awarded, it's good for 17 years.

3. *Design Patent.* This patent offers protection for a unique, ornamental design of the exterior of the product. It has nothing to do with how it works, only with how it looks. For instance, Auguste Bartholdi, the sculptor, had a design patent on the Statue of Liberty. It's not illogical to have a utility patent and a design patent on the same invention. One covers how it works. The other how it looks.

4. *Trademarks.* The U.S. Department of Commerce has a useful booklet about trademarks, which costs $1.25. Ordering information is in the Appendix. According to the booklet, "A trademark may be a word, symbol, design, or combination word and design, a slogan or even a distinctive sound which identifies the goods and services of one party from another." "Coke" and "Pepsi" are trademarks.

5. *Copyrights.* Patents and trademarks are issued by the PTO. Copyrights, on the other hand, come from the Library of Congress. That's because copyrights offer

protection for artistic and literary works. Books will merit a copyright, as will works like movies, cartoon characters, drawings, plays, songs, and so on. If you'd like to have a government publication on this subject, look in the Appendix for ordering information. A copyright is good for your lifetime, plus 50 years. Maybe a nice going away present for your heirs.

You'll Be Happier If You Leave It to Experts

If you feel your idea warrants a utility patent, don't attempt to secure it without a patent attorney. Although you can do it yourself, the patent you secure on your own may not be as ironclad as one secured through a trained professional. It's an expensive process, but a good lawyer will enable you to get all the protection your idea merits. A weak patent will be almost valueless. I am a big believer in doing everything you can on your own, without lawyers, but I would never file for a utility patent by myself. I've just read through a thick instruction book that purports to show an average person how to apply for a utility patent. The more I waded through it, the more I was convinced that this is best left in the hands of experts. It's really too important to be a do-it-yourself project. To give you a sense of what's involved, some of the basic application forms are included in the Appendix.

In 1988, 148,183 applications were received by the Patent Office and 83,595 patents were granted—a little better than 50 percent. Also, in 1988, the average waiting time to receive the patent was 19.9 months—pretty close to two years. These are not wonderful statistics, considering that even the simplest application will probably cost several thousand dollars, with no upper limit. Nevertheless, if what you've invented is valuable, it deserves the strongest patent you can get. If someone tries to bypass your idea, you'll bless the day that your patent was acquired through a competent professional.

Use It or Lose It

I don't mean to imply that you should wait the two years until you receive your patent before showing your idea to potential licensees. When your attorney makes the filing, you
should put "Patent Pending" on all your material and proceed to offer your idea in a vigorous manner. If you're going
to sit around cooling your heels until you actually have a
patent, your terrific idea might quietly become passé.

"Patent Pending" gives you no legal protection whatsoever,
since you may never actually be awarded the patent. However, if does warn everyone that an application has been
made, and when and if the patent is awarded, you'll be coming after anyone who has copied it. Competing manufacturers usually pay attention to this. They don't want to invest
thousands of dollars in tooling to knock off a product that
may become patented even before their knock-off is on the
market. But it doesn't always work that way.

Some small manufacturers automatically put "Patent Pending" on all their packages, even though no patents are ever
applied for. The hope is that it will deter the competition, but
the irony is that, since the competition does the same thing,
neither one pays any attention to the warning. Of course it's
against the law, but it's a tough law to police. Large companies would never put false "Patent Pending" warnings on
their packages, and even fast-buck companies will pause if
large tooling costs are involved.

Who in the World Needs a Design Patent?

While I urge that you use a patent attorney if you're filing for
a utility patent, there is nothing wrong in going after a design patent on your own. The process is simpler and there is
less margin for error. The filing fee is $250, and the issuance
fee is $370. The patent has a 14-year term. Design patents

aren't usually worth the expense unless the design itself is absolutely critical to the success of the product. Then, it's worth its weight in gold. Here's what I mean:

> Three companies are the major producers of those little car air fresheners that hang from rearview mirrors. Companies A and B own the licensing rights to every hot property on the market. I mean properties like Playboy and Garfield and Snoopy and Ninja Turtles. All that company C owns is a design patent on an air freshener in the shape of a pine tree. The presidents of companies A and B each told me independently that C is the leader in the business.

I mention this because it's a unique situation. For company C, their design patent is extremely valuable, it's the basis for their business. However, it's rare that the ornamental design of a product is all that important. It's not difficult to circumvent a design patent, and one design is usually as good as the next. You must be the judge as to how this applies to your own new idea.

If It's from Your Brain, Copyright It!

Most of my own new ideas qualify for copyright protection. This is something you can certainly do yourself. In fact, your original work is deemed by the government to automatically have copyright protection as soon as you create it. Nevertheless, I automatically include the copyright notification on all my original work and you should certainly do the same. You've seen it many times: it's the C in a circle with the date and the author's name (for example, © 1993, Harvey Reese). Look at the front page to see how carefully the publishing company protects the copyright for this book.

Also, although it's no longer mandatory, it's also a good idea to register your work with the United States Copyright Office. The government application form is included in the Appendix. The registration fee is only 10 dollars, and a copyright registration gives you the right to go to court to protect your property. If your work is registered before any infringement occurs, you can sue for recovery of your costs, legal fees, and damages without the necessity of proving them. These are called "Statutory Damages." Under the right circumstances, a copyright is perfect protection for your product. In the game of Monopoly, for instance, you couldn't get patent protection for the action of the game. After all, many board games involve the throwing of dice and the movement of pawns around the board. What you can protect with copyrights and trademarks is the distinctive "look" of the game. That includes the name, the design of the board, the cards, the money, the pawns—probably everything except the dice.

Name It and Claim It

Even if your product idea doesn't warrant a patent, perhaps you can give it a great name or slogan or "look." This is the kind of material you can protect with a trademark, and it can potentially add enormous value to your concept. You can't overestimate the value of a catchy name that quickly and clearly tells what your product does. If you didn't call a hula hoop a hula hoop, what else could you possibly call it?

Sophisticated marketing companies pay a great deal of attention to the names of their products because they appreciate their importance. Companies exist for the sole purpose of creating these names and command high fees for doing it. But if the name is right, many manufacturers feel it's money well spent.

One of the best known of these naming companies is Name Lab, Inc., of San Francisco. They're responsible for names such as Acura, Compaq, Geo, Lumina, and Zapmail. The people who do this kind of work call themselves "constructual linguists," and they call their company a "name development laboratory." It's quite serious work as you can see from the following paragraph about security, taken from one of Name Lab's pamphlets:

> As we routinely deal with such sensitive information as new products and corporate mergers, only Name Lab employees are admitted to our offices. We employ locked files, coded record systems, and a single copy documents policy. Reference materials are returned and project discs erased at the completion of a project.

Since companies spend so much time on this, it may pay for you to do it as well. If your product idea is just mediocre, you probably won't sell it. But if that mediocre product has a great name, a great slogan, a great look, chances are you *will* sell it. It's that simple. Without the name, the Teenage Mutant Ninja Turtles would probably just be a couple of reptiles looking for a pizza.

Under the right circumstances, copyrights and trademarks are just as important as a utility patent, and are just as vigorously defended. Here, for instance, is a typical ad in a toy trade magazine:

NOTICE
FROM
RUSS BERRIE AND COMPANY, INC.
TROLL COPYRIGHT INFRINGERS
WILL BE PROSECUTED
Russ Berrie and Company, Inc. is hereby warning anyone who infringes upon Troll copyrights owned by **Russ** that they will be prosecuted. **Russ** owns numerous copyrights for its various Trolls and Troll Kidz™ products and will vigorously enforce its rights by taking legal action and by seeking enforcement of its copyrights by U.S. customs.

Knockoffs are frequent in the toy industry, and the lawsuits fly hot and heavy. It is unlikely that a more litigious group of companies exists anywhere. One of the reasons for the many infringements may be that the selling period for fad merchandise is so brief it can come and go even before a trial date is set. The one who does the knockoff is often willing to risk either that a trial will never take place because of an out-of-court settlement or that, if there is a trial, the only penalty will be to pay a royalty to the patent or copyright owner. In the meantime, the offending firm perhaps has made a big score off the other company's creativity and can well afford to pay the legal costs. The stakes are high, and with millions of dollars on the line, the knockoff companies factor the anticipated legal costs into the selling price of the product. The consumers lose; the lawyers win. Fortunately, those of us who create and license the products are above the fray. As fiercely as the toy companies may compete with one another, I have never experienced or heard of an occasion where ideas were stolen from the people who create them. The industry pays out many millions of dollars each year in royalties and licensing fees, and is happy to do it. Why not? Every dollar paid out represents about 20 dollars taken in.

Foreign Patents

Obtaining a foreign patent involves a long, expensive, complicated process, so you shouldn't attempt to get one on your own. And you shouldn't attempt it at all unless your product idea has global significance. The United States is such a huge market by itself, and the cost to obtain and defend foreign patents is so onerous, that you should probably skip it unless you have a major sponsor behind you.

Most of the world's industrialized countries are joined by treaty in something known as the Paris Convention. Essentially, this treaty gives you the right, after filing in a member country, such as the United States, to file in another member country within one year, using the date of the original filing. For instance, let's say you applied for a patent in the United States. In the meantime, six months later, a French manufacturer learns of your product and decides to apply for a French patent. Subsequently, within the year of your U.S. filing, you also file for a French patent. Because both countries are signatories of the Paris Convention treaty, your application would take precedence over that of the French manufacturer. Conversely, if you never file outside the United States, the French manufacturer can copy your product and sell it at will throughout the rest of the world.

Various other patent organizations overlap the Paris Convention and also impact on the methods and time periods you have for making your patent application. These include the European Patent Office (EPO), the Patent Cooperative Treaty (PCT), and the African Intellectual Property Organization. While in general I have suggested that you forgo this type of protection, there are certain exceptions.

1. If the American company you license your product to has a strong overseas marketing component, it might be interested in securing foreign patent protection at its own expense. The patent would be registered in your name and licensed to the company.

2. If that mythical French manufacturer comes to you for a license, the Licensing Agreement could specify that the company will secure a French (or European) patent in your name, to be licensed to it. Or you could secure the patent on your own, subject to the execution of a satisfactory licensing arrangement with the French manufacturer.

The Perils of Joint Ownership

If the product was invented jointly by you and your brother-in-law, Melvin, you will file for the patent as co-inventors.

The PTO doesn't care whether you did 90 percent of the work and Melvin did 10 percent. As far as the government is concerned, you are each equal inventors and can act independently of each other in selling or licensing your patent. It doesn't take much imagination to envision the problems that can develop from such an arrangement. Each of you could actually wind up competing with the other to license the invention and keep all the royalties. It's all perfectly legal.

There are two obvious solutions. The first is to have a presubmission contract that spells out how the two of you will proceed. The second, and better, solution is not to have a partner at all.

It's a natural tendency for people to look for partners whenever they embark on a new venture. There's comfort in having someone to share the problems with, and it gives many people the courage to press forward. However, you have to confront the reality that almost every partnership eventually fails, usually with bitterness on both sides. Look at your own circle of friends, and you'll see what I mean. I've had partners twice in my career and both times it ended unpleasantly, not because my partners were bad or dishonest people, but simply because it's virtually inevitable that friction will develop when every decision must be made in concert. So if you really don't need Melvin's help, you're much better off by yourself. (If you must have companionship, I suggest you get a pet.)

A Pet Is Better than a Partner

Now that we know something about the legal protection that's available, let's look at how much we can do without it.

HOW TO GET SOLID PROTECTION FOR YOUR IDEAS WITHOUT PAYING LEGAL FEES

First of all, keep your notes. They should be dated and filed in order. Then make a detailed drawing of your final design, date it, and have it witnessed by two people who have no stake in it. Take one copy and safely file it away. Take another copy and mail it to yourself. Don't open the letter! For the price of a stamp, you will have a postmark that provides some evidence as to when you conceived the idea. Every patent lawyer I spoke to advised me that this old trick of sending a letter to yourself doesn't mean much in court because letters can so easily be tampered with. I understand this, but it's such an easy thing to do, and coupled with your other proofs, it adds to the preponderance of the evidence identifying your invention.

Whatever Else You Do, Do This

Also, for six dollars, you can file a disclosure form with the Patent and Trademark Office in Washington, D.C. Just send your check along with a detailed description, drawings, and/ or photos of your product design. Your pages should be numbered and no larger than $8^1/_2 \times 13$ inches. If you include a self-addressed, stamped envelope, the PTO will send you back a Disclosure Document Number. The Department will keep your disclosure on file for two years. It is not passing judgment on the merit of your submission, but is providing proof as to the date of its conception. A usable form is reproduced in the Appendix. The Disclosure Document Number, the witnessed copies of your drawings, and the sealed, post-marked envelope are like triple locks for your product idea. The total cost will probably be less than 10 dollars.

You should also keep an accurate record of your expenses (including this book). If you act like an inventor and keep notes like an inventor, the government may consider you to be in the inventing business. As such, your expenses will probably be deductible by filing a Schedule "C" with your tax return. Your own accountant can guide you. Also, the Appendix provides a list of inventor organizations. You may wish to join one and avail yourself of the tax guidance and information that members receive.

The Paper Trail

Courts usually find that if you present a new and novel idea to a company—something that wouldn't be obvious in its normal course of business—the firm has an obligation to keep the information confidential and to not use it, or profit from it, without your permission. This is not hard-and-fast law, but judges will almost always find in your favor if you run into an unscrupulous company. To a large extent, it will depend on the nature of the information you disclose.

Suppose you saw a survey that said most women prefer turquoise over every other color. And suppose you went to a steam iron manufacturer with the idea that they change the color of the handles on their irons to turquoise. If a year or so later, the company actually did switch to turquoise, that doesn't mean you could collect royalties on the sale of every new steam iron. Your "idea" would never fit the court's definition of being new and novel, the color preferences of women is certainly something a company could be expected to determine in its normal course of business. However, if what you presented was an altogether new type of handle that could be switched around to accommodate either left- or right-handed users, and if the company simply took your idea, the courts would almost certainly find in your favor.

To protect against such thefts, you must establish proof that it was your idea to begin with and that you introduced the idea to the manufacturer on a specified date. You do this by developing what lawyers call a "paper trail." For instance, if you had a meeting with Franklin Smedley to show your new Switcheroo Handle, you'd send off the following letter after your appointment.

Dear Mr. Smedley:

It was very nice meeting you today. I appreciate your courtesy and am quite pleased with your initial favorable reaction to my SWITCHEROO HANDLE concept for your steam iron line.

I am herewith enclosing the samples and drawings listed below for your internal discussion, and as you suggested, I'll call you in two weeks.

Sincerely,

If Mr. Smedley said he did not like your new product idea, and maybe threw you bodily out of his office, you should send off a letter like this:

Dear Mr. Smedley:

It was nice meeting you today, and I appreciated the opportunity to present my SWITCHEROO HANDLE concept for your consideration. I was sorry to learn that it doesn't fit into your current marketing plans, but I certainly understand your reasoning.

I thank you again for your courtesy and hope my next new product concept will be more suitable to your needs.

Sincerely,

Mr. Smedley will understand that you didn't send him one of these letters just because your mother taught you such good manners. He'll realize that he's dealing with someone who knows the legal implications of the letter and he will understand that it is like a warning shot across the bow.

And if Smedley calls you for some additional information, his mail tomorrow should include another letter from you:

> Dear Franklin (by now you're on a first name basis):
>
> Thank you for your telephone call today. Now that I've had the time to reflect on your question, I'm more convinced than ever that the answer I gave you is correct. The framus will fit snugly on the thigmetz if you loosen the witzberg.
>
> Please call me again if I can be helpful. In the meantime, I'm still scheduled to call you next Thursday to see if you plan to proceed with my SWITCHEROO HANDLE concept for your steam iron line.
>
> > Cordially,

In other words, every contact you have with Mr. Smedley should be followed by a confirming letter. Make sure you keep a copy for yourself. Also, keep a copy of your phone bills that reflect any long distance calls made to Mr. Smedley, or travel expenses to his office. If the need ever arises, you'll be able to completely document your dealings with that potential archfiend, Franklin Smedley.

For a modest investment, you can have letterheads and business cards printed. This not only will make your dealings with Smedley more professional but may prove quite beneficial when it comes time to pay your taxes. It would also be a good idea to set up a special checking account to pay any expenses you might incur for items such as travel, prototypes, artwork, and photography.

I automatically create a paper trail, even with companies I've been dealing with for years. I've never had a problem, and I'm sure that it's partly because everything I do is documented. Gypsy Rose Lee said, "God is love, but have it in writing." If you hope for the best while you prepare for the worst, you'll never be caught off guard.

WHEN YOU REALLY DO NEED A LAWYER, HERE'S HOW TO FIND THE RIGHT ONE

Patent attorney fees can be quite expensive, so you should try to evaluate your new idea as frankly as possible to determine if the expense is warranted. If you decide you do need a lawyer, keep in mind that it's just another service business and you're a customer. Act like one. Shop, negotiate, ask questions.

First of all, as obvious as this sounds, only use a patent attorney who knows what you're talking about. Patent attorneys, like doctors, often tend to specialize. If your invention involves complicated chemical matters, you probably will not want to work with an attorney who specializes in mechanically engineered products. Most patent attorneys are also engineers of one kind or another, so you may want to ask what degrees your attorney has. And don't go to Uncle Bernie, who is a personal injury lawyer, just because he says he'll cut you a deal on the price. You'll just be spending your money buying him an education. Patent law is a highly technical speciality, and you need somebody who can understand and perhaps offer suggestions to improve your concept. Can your uncle Bernie do that?

Develop your list of potential patent lawyers from recommendations from friends, from your regular attorney, from inventor organizations, and from the telephone book. If you still haven't found someone you feel comfortable with, the PTO can supply you with a directory of more than 13,000 individuals whom they have authorized to act on behalf of inventors. To qualify, the attorneys must have the appropriate legal training and also a college degree in engineering or a physical science.

Don't Worry, Lawyers Don't Gossip

When you call an attorney to make an initial appointment, the very first question to ask is whether there will be a charge for the preliminary meeting. If you spend time having the attorney review your product, it's fair that he should charge you something, but if your conversation is limited to a discussion of fees, rates, and billing methods, no money should change hands. You shouldn't have to pay a fee for asking what the fee is.

An attorney can only quote a price by knowing the exact nature of your invention, so be prepared to reply fully to the questions he or she might ask. Patent attorneys are bound by law to keep what you tell them confidential, so you needn't be concerned.

How Long Is a Five-Minute Call?

In addition to learning the attorney's hourly rate, you'll also want to find out the minimum billable unit. Let's say you interview two attorneys, each of whom bills at $160 per hour. Attorney A has a minimum billable unit of 15 minutes, and attorney B's is 6 minutes. If you make a 5-minute telephone call to each of them, attorney A will bill you for $40 ($1/4$ of $160), and attorney B will bill you for $16 ($1/10$ of $160). In my experience, most attorneys use the 6-minute system, so be properly alerted if you meet one who uses 15-minute units.

Since an attorney is going to bill you for *everything*, you must keep a log and organize your thoughts before making phone calls or keeping appointments. Plan your meetings: Have a list of the questions you want answered and be concise and to the point. It's been my experience that attorneys make great listeners. They're happy to hear your jokes and funny stories, but you have a very expensive audience. Talk may be cheap, but not when you're dealing with an attorney. The clock starts ticking as soon as you walk through the door and doesn't stop until you exit. So do it as quickly as you reasonably can. And be sure you clearly understand what a procedure is going to cost before your attorney undertakes it. There shouldn't be any surprises. This is simply common sense and should not cause a professional to take offense.

Beware of the "G" Word

If you call in a building contractor to remodel your basement, you'll receive an estimate for material, labor, and fixtures, as well as a tentative schedule. You'll compare several contractors and finally make your choice. Dealing with a patent attorney is quite similar, and you should use similar judgment. Ask the several attorneys you meet with to break down their charges, which they'll be happy to do, and then you can make an intelligent decision. These are the likely components:

1. The search.
2. Government filing fees.
3. Drawings (number of views required).
4. Out-of-pocket expenses.
5. Professional services.

Based on my own experience, which I have confirmed with patent attorney acquaintances, the fees quoted for the first 4 components will not vary much from attorney to attorney. They shouldn't because they all represent services the attorney purchases on your behalf. However, on the 5th component (professional services), you'll receive an incredible range of charges. For instance, if you check with four attorneys, the highest quoted cost for professional services may actually be twice as high as the lowest quoted cost. When I ask why this is so, nobody seems to know. No one would dare suggest that the higher price will get you a correspondingly higher level of service. After all, it's only a simple patent application. Could it be that they're afraid to say the "G" word? Could it be that greed has something to do with it?

One attorney told me that she used to work for a prestigious patent firm, which prided itself on being the highest priced firm in the East (or maybe in the country, I don't remember). Anyway, if another firm raised its hourly rate to match those prices, this firm would automatically raise its rates even higher.

While I'm not suggesting that you automatically give your work to the cheapest attorney, I am submitting that higher cost does not necessarily relate to a higher quality of work. When all is said and done, it's still a judgment call and, if the fees are within your budget, you should deal with the attorney with whom you're most comfortable. Both you and the attorney hope that this is the beginning of a long relationship, so it's important above all else that you like the individual's personality and respect his or her ability.

The first patent attorney I ever used was one I bought by price alone, which turned out to be a big mistake. His hourly rate was about $20 less than the nearest next quote, but I probably overpaid by $1,000 before I was finished because he was inept and greedy. I say he was inept because he had to "research" simple facts, thereby wasting an hour here and an hour there. I say he was greedy because he padded the bill with petty charges. His secretary called once to ask for my birth date to put on a form. The call lasted about 25 seconds. My monthly bill reflected this as a half-hour "telephone conference with client." Obviously, I never used him again, and I learned a few years later that he was no longer with the firm. Fired I hope. So, yes, definitely check out the pricing, but make sure you pick an attorney with some intelligence and some class.

It Never Hurts to Ask

While we're on the subject of fees, if the price quoted is more than you can afford, it's quite appropriate to ask if the attorney can come down a bit. Please don't be embarrassed. It's a legitimate question, and you may be pleasantly surprised at the results. Lawyers are, after all, in business, and they don't want to see you walk out the door any more than a retailer wants to see you leave the shop empty-handed. Once the fees are settled, what about the terms? If you can live with the attorney's regular payment system, fine. If you can't, that's also negotiable, and I promise you won't be the first client to get better prices or extended terms.

Money considerations aside for a moment, should you use a large firm or a single practitioner? The large firm has specialists in virtually every discipline, so no matter how complicated your concept is, someone there will understand it. If the single attorney gets stuck, whom does he turn to? On the other hand, you're probably such a small fry for the large firm that you'll wind up with a youngster who still hasn't had time to get his law degree framed. The single practitioner may not have a back-up staff, but perhaps he has ten years of experience under his belt. But is he so small because he's not good?

Would You Like to Be a Loss Leader?

My own instinct usually leads me to a medium-size firm. Patent firms tend to be much smaller than the giant corporate forms, so "medium-size" means approximately a six-lawyer group. On the rare occasions when I use a patent attorney, I usually stay away from the extremes. I feel the single practitioner may be trying to do too many things alone to take care of my needs properly, and I don't want to be the big company's smallest client. A senior partner with a large firm recently confided that they lose money with individual inventors. They only take them on because they hope they'll grow into larger accounts. That probably represents the thinking of most large firms, which reconfirms my feelings that I'm better off with a smaller group. I don't know about you, but I don't want to be anybody's loss leader.

Would You Like Your Lawyer as Your Partner?

Sometimes, if your concept is patentable and particularly appealing, an attorney may be willing to provide services free in return for a percentage of your potential profits. Because of having a proprietary interest in your success, the attorney might be willing to provide leads and introductions and could give advice and lend expertise to the negotiation and contractual dealings with the licensee.

Some patent attorneys tell me that such an arrangement would violate the bar's code of ethics. The reasoning is that an attorney presumably has much more knowledge of patents and licensing than a layperson; hence, an unscrupulous professional can take unfair advantage of a naive inventor. There's a great deal of merit to this reasoning, and you should be fairly warned. I know for a fact, however, that some professional inventors do have such an ongoing relationship with their attorneys. If the attorney is trustworthy, as most are, and if the inventor is sophisticated, this kind of relationship could be mutually beneficial. If the stakes are large and require substantial legal work, this option is worth considering. The decision depends on your own financial situation, the complexity of the idea, and the degree of confidence you have in yourself. Some attorneys will be willing to discuss an arrangement like this, and others won't. If you're interested, it can't hurt to ask.

What Happens When You Meet with Your Attorney?

Before your first visit, you must take the time to clearly write out the nature of your invention, supporting the description, if possible, with sketches and a model. You want to be sure that your attorney clearly understands from the outset the exact nature of your invention, its basis, and the existence of any past or present competition. You want to be thorough, and you want to be clear. But you don't want to make an oration. Remember that the clock is ticking, so have everything in order before you enter the office, and stick to the point while you're there. In conducting research for your invention, you will have undoubtedly discovered information about other products similar to yours that may be on the market now, or were so in the past. Whatever you know that's pertinent should be conveyed to your attorney to save time and aid in research on your behalf.

Your attorney, after carefully reviewing all your material, and possibly conducting some preliminary research, will tell you one of three things:

1. *Your Idea Is, er, Shall We Say, "Prehistoric."* In the attorney's judgment, your idea isn't workable and/or is not sufficiently novel to earn a patent. As with a doctor, you can go elsewhere for a second opinion, but I don't recommend it. If you are told that your idea isn't patentable, I suggest you should accept that as fact. There's no incentive for an attorney to tell you that if it isn't true.

2. *Your Idea Is, Dare I Suggest, "Pedestrian."* The attorney may advise that, although it is possible to obtain a patent, it won't have much value because your invention isn't very profound. Lawyers boast that they can get a patent of one sort or another for almost every

"Your Idea Is, er, Shall We Say 'Prehistoric'"

invention placed on their desk. They call these "red button" patents because, if nothing else, they can get a patent for the red button you used to start your gizmo. If all they can get for you is a weak patent, you might as well save your money. Most lawyers will volunteer this information. If they don't, it's your job to ask.

3. *Your Invention Is, How Shall I Put It, "Fantastic!"* The attorney, after saying that your invention appears to have considerable merit, and that it should be possible to get a broad, solid patent, will undoubtedly recommend a patent search to see if someone else has beaten you to the punch.

Whatever opinion the attorney gives you about your idea, bear in mind that the evaluation is strictly a legal one, and the attorney is not necessarily passing judgment on its commercial value. Just because the attorney may say the idea isn't patentable does not have to mean that the idea won't have considerable commercial value to the right company. Conversely, if the attorney says he can get an iron-clad patent for your idea, that still doesn't mean the marketplace is anxiously awaiting its introduction.

In other words, the attorney's expert legal opinion is neither cause to despair nor rejoice. It's only a step along your way.

THE PATENT SEARCH

There's no law that says you have to conduct a search before applying for a patent, but it's so sensible to proceed in this manner that almost everyone does it. A search is much less expensive than a patent filing, so it's logical to first make sure that your idea hasn't already been taken. And if it has, when you see the existing patent you may be able to redesign a way around it. Either way you're ahead. So, assuming you're going to proceed in this manner, there are three routes you can take:

1. Engage your patent attorney to conduct the search.
2. Hire a professional patent search company.
3. Do the work yourself.

Engage Your Patent Attorney to Do the Search

Your attorney is not going to the library to personally research the patents; he or she is going to use the same kind of patent search company that you can hire on your own. Ask both your attorney and the search company what they'll charge. If the difference is small, you might as well have your attorney handle it so he can control the whole process. If the difference is significant, there's no sense in spending money needlessly. An attorney usually marks up his costs by 40 percent, so I'd be surprised if the savings weren't substantial by dealing directly with the search firm. What constitutes "substantial savings?" You'll have to be the judge after you weigh all the factors.

Hire a Professional Patent Search Firm

You can find patent search companies in your telephone directory, by networking with other inventors, and from inventor organizations. A visit to your local telephone company office will get you access to a Washington, D.C., classified directly where you'll find all the names you'll need. To give you an idea of costs, a professional searcher charges in the range of $50 per hour, and it will take the searcher less than a day to complete a search on a simple mechanical patent. The average is 5 hours. One note of caution. In using the phone book, it's easy to confuse a patent search firm with a patent marketing firm since they both offer searches. Question them closely before you award the assignment.

Do the Work Yourself

You should definitely consider the third option—doing it yourself—if you have the time and access to a patent library (see Appendix for addresses). The average search takes a nonprofessional about 15 hours. It's an absorbing process, and the libraries have well-trained attendants to help you. In visiting the depository in my city, I have been quite impressed with the facilities and the caliber of the people who offered assistance. Many of the inventions themselves are so interesting that you could easily spend hours just browsing through them.

Most of the attorneys I consulted advised that it's beneficial for the inventor to conduct the patent search himself for a simple invention. It's interesting, informative, and well within the average layperson's capabilities. It's best to do it at the main Patent Office in Crystal City, Virginia, because you can handle copies of the actual patents. However, if that's too far away, official patent depositories are located throughout the country, so perhaps you'll find one nearby. The addresses are listed in the Appendix.

The patent files are divided into five main categories: Electrical, Mechanical, Chemical, Plant, and Design. Each of these categories has its own classifications and subclassifications. There are more than 400 classes and more than 120,000 subclasses. But don't be daunted; it's all computerized, and the attendants will see you through it.

APPLYING FOR THE UTILITY PATENT

Assuming that the search uncovers nothing to conflict with your concept, your lawyer will now open your file and apply for the patent. You can now properly identify all your material as "Patent Pending" and should be proceeding with your licensing efforts while your application is going through the approval process. Be assured that the application for your patent, even if it's rejected, is held in strict confidence by the Patent Office. The public can never see it. Once a patent has been issued, however, anyone can get a copy by sending in the patent number and $1.50.

Without taking you through the application step by step, in essence, you will give your lawyer the power of attorney to act on your behalf in filing a standard patent application with the PTO. The attorney will clearly and precisely explain your invention, supported by drawings that have been rendered by a patent draftsperson, who is familiar with the style and manner required by the PTO. Your attorney will explain what your idea is, what it does, and how it advances the state of the art in the invention's field. Up to this point, the work could probably be done by a paralegal. Where your attorney earns a fee is in the statement of the claims.

The First Action

The claims, listed one after the other, are what are proposed to be unique and exclusive to your invention. These are the points that you're asking the PTO to give to you and you alone for the next 17 years. Your attorney is going to attempt to make these claims as broad as possible, while the PTO examiner will attempt to keep them as narrow as possible. This is the difference between a good and bad patent. If the patent is too narrow, competitors can more easily bypass it. If it's broad and sweeping in its exclusivity, your patent is more valuable and will, perhaps, greatly improve your ability to license your invention.

Your claims will be reviewed by an examiner who will search through the appropriate existing and expired patents and available literature to assure that your invention is truly new. The examiner's decision, called a "first action," will be sent to your attorney:

1. The examiner may conclude that your idea is not new or novel and may therefore deny the patent.

2. The examiner may accept all the claims as submitted, and your application will be passed through for patent issuance (assuming you pay the appropriate fees).

3. The examiner may accept some of the claims you make for your invention and reject others.

If you conducted a search beforehand, and if your idea passed through your attorney's informal screening, there's a good chance that it won't be rejected out of hand. There's also a good chance that your claims won't be accepted complete, as presented. The most common action is to allow some claims and not allow others. Your attorney, after determining the case that can be made, will respond with evidence to support the original claims. The examiner may revise the decision or not, and the correspondence may go back and forth several times. At some point, however, the examiner proclaims the decision to be final and the last course open is an appeal to the Patents Commissioner. The examiners' decisions are rarely reversed, and this final step should only be considered if the stakes are high and if you feel you have an exceptionally strong case to be made. Keep in mind that it's a time-consuming process and you're paying your attorney by the hour.

Assuming all the claims are eventually settled and the patent is issued, you will be expected to pay an issuance fee of $280, plus maintenance fees at various intervals. You won't receive an invoice from the government, so it's up to you to know that these fees are due within $3^1/_2$ years, $7^1/_2$ years, and 11 years from the date of the patent's issuance. If you don't pay the fees, your patent will expire prematurely.

However, before you even retain an attorney, it's worth the few dollars to get the government booklets on patents, trademarks, and copyrights. I've only touched on the subject here, and the booklets are quite comprehensive. They can help you determine how much you can do yourself. It's probably a great deal more than you think. And even if you do engage an attorney, the more you know about the process, the better a client you'll be.

Invention Marketing Companies Will Break Your Heart

If you look up *Patent Attorneys* and *Patent Searches* in your telephone directory, you'll probably also notice listings for the dreaded invention marketing companies. Most of them will take your money and run like a thief in the night. Such companies prey on novice inventors by offering market research, patent search, patent applications, manufacturer submissions, and license negotiations. I've had no firsthand experience with invention marketing companies, but I've heard and read enough horror stories to strongly advise you to stay clear of them. The first thing they'll want is a retainer, and you shouldn't pay a retainer to anybody, particularly to anyone in an industry with as many corrupt operators as this one.

The idea is that you tell such companies about your invention, in general terms, and for a modest sum, a few hundred dollars, they agree to do "market research" on the sales potential of your idea. Naturally, the report raves about the "enormous" market there is for your invention and implies that only a genius could have created it. That the report is canned, gleaned from thousands of other previous reports, seems almost beside the point. The victim is now excited and hopeful enough to willingly pay thousands of dollars for all the other services. Finally, when the string runs out and there are no more services to be sold, the inventor is a little wiser and a whole lot poorer for the experience.

A California invention company, when forced to open its books by the Attorney General of the State, revealed that of all the thousands and thousands of people who paid for services over the years, only three individuals made a profit from the association. In a spirit of fair play, I offered to interview a principal from one of these companies, to hear his side of the story. The only answer I received was a runaround. The man I spoke to (most of these are franchised operations) said he was "too busy" to see me. I asked if he could at least send me some of his literature. He promised he would, but of course nothing ever arrived.

I don't mean to suggest that these companies are operating illegally, because they're not. In a literal sense they do exactly as they promise. The problem is that it's all smoke and mirrors and, as the money is gently extracted, the inventor's hopes and dreams are seldom, if ever, realized.

If you can't resist the siren call, check first with the Better Business Bureau and ask the company to give you the names of at least six current clients.

Invention marketing companies should not be confused with backers, venture capitalists, and licensing agents. These people will sponsor or represent you in one way or another because they believe in your idea. Their remuneration is a percentage of whatever royalties your idea generates. If it's not successfully licensed or marketed, they get nothing. Invention marketing companies, on the other hand, earn their money from the fees you pay them for services rendered.

Don't Forget about Angels

If you have confidence in your idea, but lack the funds to retain an attorney to see it through, you might want to give some thought to getting a backer. Not a partner, a backer. In exchange for funding the legal and miscellaneous costs, the backer receives a portion of the net profits. It's your invention, and you call the shots. The percentage for the backer is negotiable. If I were doing it, I'd offer my backer 25 percent, and I'd be willing to go up to a third. That's purely subjective, and your input is as valid as mine. The backer would be investing in you in the same way an angel invests in a Broadway show. Neither has a voice in the management, and the only time they should make an appearance is when there are profits to divvy up. If my circumstances dictated the need for financing, I would have no qualms about trying to arrange this kind of deal. Keeping 100 percent of nothing is still nothing.

Before leaving the subject of patents and inventions, I'd like to tell you a little bit about a very interesting organization: *The National Inventors Hall of Fame.*

The United States is the most inventingest country the world has ever seen. Ideas are born in our nation's workshops and laboratories that affect the well-being of every living creature on earth. In any area of endeavor, a few individuals manage to reach much greater heights than their associates. The field of invention is no exception, and so to honor these superstars, the idea of the National Inventors Hall of Fame was conceived.

Angels Come in All Shapes and Sizes

When you consider what the inventor inductees into this institution have accomplished, you must wonder what life in our society would have been like if they hadn't existed. The Hall of Fame's parent organization, the National Invention Center, was officially born in 1973 and is sponsored in part by the U.S. Patent and Trademark Office and the National Council of Patent Law Attorneys. To quote from the organization's literature:

> The National Inventors Hall Of Fame is dedicated to the individuals who conceived the great technological advances which this nation fosters through its patent system. The purpose of The Hall is to honor these inventors and bring public recognition to them and to their contributions to the nation's welfare.

The National Invention Center sponsors "Camp Invention" at 25 locations throughout the country, in an effort to get youngsters in grades 1 through 6 excited about science, technology, and the arts. They also sponsor a Collegiate Inventors Competition with cash awards for students and their sponsors. In 1991, they had 104 qualifying entries from 47 colleges and universities.

In addition, the National Invention Center sponsors seminars and other activities for patent attorneys and interested laypeople. If you'd like literature or more information about this worthwhile, nonprofit organization, contact:

> The National Invention Center
> 80 West Bowery, Suite 201
> Akron, OH 44308
> Phone (216) 762-4463/Fax (216) 762-6313

In making our way through the CRASH Course, so far we've looked at ways to help you create your million-dollar idea, we've explored ways to determine its value, and we've examined legal and practical ways to protect it. So far, it's been an uphill fight. Now begins the payoff process: Your new idea is ready to meet the world. In the next chapter, we'll discuss how to prepare it for its debut.

It's time for the "A" in our program. It's time for Action. Now we go on the attack.

4

SWING INTO ACTION

Prospecting, Getting the Appointment, and Preparing the Presentation

Before anything else, getting ready is the secret of success.

—Henry Ford

About 50 years ago, so the legend goes, a teenage beauty named Lana Turner was sipping a soda in a drugstore at the corner of Hollywood and Vine, when a big-time director came up and offered to put her in pictures. That probably was the last time in history anyone ever succeeded by simply being discovered. Today, you have to push and hustle and yell "Look at me!" if you want to get anywhere. A mediocre idea that has been successfully licensed is a thousand times better than a brilliant invention that's gathering dust on a shelf, waiting to be discovered. An old saying reminds us, "Nothing happens until somebody sells something."

In referring to the idea for his stores, Frank W. Woolworth once remarked that he was the world's worst salesman and, therefore, he had to make his stores a place where it was easy for people to buy. You may feel you're ready to challenge Mr. Woolworth for that title, which is exactly why you must spend the time to prepare a professional, persuasive presentation. Think of it as your store, and, like Woolworth's, its purpose is to make it easy for people to buy your idea.

HOW TO SHAPE UP YOUR IDEA FOR PRESENTATION: IT'S NOT IMPORTANT UNLESS IT LOOKS IMPORTANT

As the scene opens, showing the interior of a chic Park Avenue café, you are seated at a quiet table with Max Dubois, president of Global Amalgamated Things, Ltd. "Max," you say, as the waiter deposits the second round of perfect Rob Roys, "I have this little idea to show you. I think you'll find it amusing."

You take your Meisterstuck Mont Blanc pen from the inside pocket of your Yves St. Laurent jacket and quickly sketch a simple design on a cocktail napkin. The ink smears on the damp paper, but the design is still barely legible in the dim café light. With a look of greedy anticipation on his face, Max deposits his Havana Luxo in the ashtray, puts down his drink, leans over and, with pudgy trembling fingers, extracts the napkin from your hand.

The second hand takes several laps around your Rolex Oyster as Max studies your drawing. People pass by the table and extend greetings to him. He simply waves them off, his beady eyes never leaving the napkin. Finally, he mutters half aloud, half to himself, "Genius. Pure genius." He reaches into his pocket, extracting a Hermes eelskin wallet and checkbook holder. "I must have it." he says. "Just name your price. I must have it."

Fade to black.

In real life, you'll probably never go on the town with Max, let alone share perfect Rob Roys with him. But if you're going to sell a new product concept to his company, chances are good that he'll see your presentation. And he's not going to buy it if it's on a cocktail napkin. So creating a professional presentation for your idea is as important as any other single step in the selling process.

Dreams Don't Open Checkbooks

The problem is that you're selling a dream and your customer doesn't buy dreams, but rather invests in reality. That's how the president acquired the big desk and the fancy office. The solution is to create a proposal that presents your idea as if it *were* reality. What you must present to your customer is *virtual* reality. The right presentation will say:

- Here's a picture showing what my product will look like when it's produced.
- Here's a model that shows how my product will work when it's produced.
- Here's a drawing showing how my product will be packaged when its produced.
- Here is research showing how many you can sell when it's produced.
- Here are estimates showing how much profit you can make when it's produced.

I could easily add a dozen more entries to this list, but I'm sure you get the point. If you're customer buys reality, you need to sell reality. To the extent that your presentation can create that illusion, it will be your principal tool in closing the deal.

"They Stopped Laughing When I Took Out My Little List"

Here's a little tip for writing your presentation. In teaching my night school course, I noticed a phenomenon that actually made me laugh out loud when I saw it for the first time. Now I just expect it. I can stand in front of the class (all adults) and talk nonstop for 45 minutes and just get glassy-eyed stares. I can be revealing the wisdom of the ages or just giving a weather report. No matter, the unblinking looks remain. However, as soon as I say something like, "There are five steps in developing an idea," or "Here are the four important things to remember when making a presentation," all notebooks are thrown open and everybody reaches for their pens.

So my tip of the day is: *Everybody Loves Lists!* Smart people love lists and so do foolish people, and rich people and poor people, and big people and little people. Every person who can read loves lists for the following five reasons:

1. Lists are easy to read.
2. Lists seem efficient.
3. Lists seem factual.
4. Lists seem to the point.
5. Lists seem conclusive.

When I say "lists," I should make it clear that I'm including all the shorthand ways to make a point. That includes pie charts, bar charts, horizontal graphs, and vertical graphs, and any other visual aid you can think of. *U.S.A. TODAY* has been living off the phenomenon for years. List lovers are everywhere. They're indistinguishable by sex, class, color, financial status, or birth sign. All of us are suckers for lists. So when you're structuring your own presentation, it's easy to organize it with headings like:

-   Five Reasons Consumers Will Buy This New Product
-   Three Reasons This New Product Will Decrease Your Production Costs
-   Eight Advantages This New Product Has over Existing Competition

The briefer your proposal, the better the chances it will be read. And if they read nothing else, they'll almost definitely look at your charts and lists.

The Cost of the Written Proposal

The basis of your proposal is an intelligent explanation of what the product is, how it works, who it benefits, and what's in it for the prospective licensee. If practical, your written presentation should also offer suggestions as to how your product should be produced, where it should be produced, what it will cost, what it can be sold for, where it should be sold, how it should be packaged, and how it should be displayed. Anything you can answer with authority should be addressed in your report. If you're just guessing about something, leave it out. And whatever you do, don't lie. You're dealing with professionals who will almost certainly uncover the fib, and that will cast a pall over everything else you've written.

The proposal will be much better if it includes attractive, full-color drawings or professionally taken color photographs to support the written exposition. And the proposal will be best if it includes a three-dimensional model or prototype, plus the supporting drawings or photographs along with the written material. If you can put something three-dimensional in the prospect's hands, it turns a dream into something practical. It turns it into virtual reality. Something that a manufacturer can hold in his hands turns a dream into salable goods.

Out of the Twilight Zone and into the Profit Zone

I only create consumer products, so everything I license ultimately ends up in a retail store. As part of my presentation, I always include a mock-up package, complete with illustrations and copy. When I put it into the licensee's hands, we stop dealing in dreams and start dealing with visible reality. I even provide drawings to show how my product will look when it's displayed in a store, and the licensee *always* lingers over that image. We're now on the customer's turf: packaging, displays, merchandising. By the strength of my visual presentation, I've managed to move my product concept out of the Twilight Zone and into the marketplace where a meeting of the minds can take place. The signing of the license is now a mere formality. Yes, a slight exaggeration, but I know you take my point.

If your product idea is truly inferior, no fancy presentation is going to help. And if your idea's truly brilliant, you may actually be able to sell it from a cocktail napkin. But most of our ideas fall someplace in between, and we need all the help we can get. We need the slickest presentation we can make. Here is what a slick presentation will do:

1. *A Slick-Looking Presentation Shows Respect for the Idea.* A crudely prepared presentation implies a lack of confidence in the idea and exposes you as an amateur. A presentation that looks special makes the idea seem special. Even the most sophisticated executives will pause longer over an attractive presentation than they will over a crude one.

2. *A Slick Presentation Makes You Look Good.* When executives see a professional presentation, they are going to pay a lot more attention to what you're telling them. After looking at the presentation, they'll look at you with greater respect.

3. *A Slick Presentation Removes Uncertainty.* Businesspeople hate uncertainty. It makes them nervous and it makes them hesitant. A slick presentation chases away fears and doubts and makes the executive more interested in moving forward. A slick presentation

edges the new product proposal a bit closer to the "sure thing" side.

4. *A Slick Presentation Will Stand on Its Own Merits.* Your visual presentation perhaps will be shown to others in your absence, so it must work by itself without you being there to say things like "And this little bump is supposed to mean. . . . "

This Is the Time to Take Your Best Shot

You'll probably have to spend some money here, but it's well worth it. The written portion of your proposal should be professionally typed or produced on a word processor. Find an artist to make the drawings, use a professional photographer, and if you can't do it yourself, get a model maker to do the prototype. A possible source of help would be a local inventors' club; another might be the head of the industrial design department at a local art college. This person can put you in touch with a bright, talented student who'll be happy to work with you. It's good experience for the student, and obviously beneficial for you. He's entitled to be paid, but it'll cost far less than if done by a professional design firm. You may even want to consider a videotape presentation. It can be quite impressive if it's applicable to your product. The obvious drawback is that the licensee may have to take it home to view it. Not every office has a VCR. This method of showing concepts has become so prevalent in the toy field that virtually every marketing executive has a VCR set up in his/her office. We are in a video age and if you can make your idea come to life on a video screen, you have an awfully powerful sales tool. What could be a more effective way to turn a dream into virtual reality? Lately, presenters have also started using toy Viewmasters (Tyco Toy) to graphically show their product ideas. They're inexpensive—about three dollars—and disposable. It's something to explore if it works for your idea.

If do you hire a professional artist to draw your product and/or a professional model maker to create a prototype requiring the use of confidential information, it would be prudent to have them sign a simple nondisclosure form before you turn over your material. Specialists like this are accustomed to signing these forms, so you can expect them to do it as a matter of course. A sample for your use is in the Appendix.

One reason franchises are so popular is that they remove so much decision making from the prospect. The franchiser's proposal spells everything out in infinite detail. The presumption is that by simply following directions, the franchisee will make a fortune. Every question is answered; every doubt is calmed. Your presentation should attempt to do the same thing. If you've answered all the questions about your product's benefits and costs, and if you've shown what profit can be made from it, all that's left for the licensee to do is nod in agreement. And nothing would make that person happier.

So make sure you have a first-class presentation. If you still can't sell your idea, at least you'll be comforted that you gave it your best shot. And if you do sell it, the money you spent on the presentation will have been more than worth your investment.

PRIORITIZING YOUR PROSPECT LIST MAY BE THE DIFFERENCE BETWEEN A BIG AND MEDIOCRE SUCCESS

I hate to have to tell you this, but it's almost impossible to sell a new product idea through an unsolicited mailing to someone who doesn't know you. I've tried more than a dozen times over the years and have never been successful. And I don't know anyone else who has been successful. I won't say it can't happen, but it's extremely rare. If your invention is compelling to a manufacturer, and if you can successfully convey that urgency in a letter, I suppose you can achieve a sale by mail. Most of our ideas, unfortunately, aren't that powerful, and they have to be sold in person.

I'm always meeting people who want to get into the mail-order business. It sounds so great. Place a little ad for a weight-reducing elixir in *U.S.A. Today* and get bundles of checks in the mail. Many inventors feel the same way. Get a patent, send form letters out to a bunch of manufacturers, and sit back and sort through the contract proposals. Have you ever met anyone who got rich through mail order? And have you ever met anyone who received money by sending out an unsolicited product proposal? If you have, then you and I don't travel with the same kind of people.

I can't stress enough the importance of personal selling versus mail solicitations. Invention marketing companies, for a fee, promise to introduce your new product idea to "hundreds of industry leaders." All they do is make a mailing from bought lists. Big deal. Company executives accustomed to getting these mailings frequently don't even open the envelopes.

Kit Carson Says You Shouldn't Become a Statistic

Yesterday I had a meeting in New York to present a new product idea to a major textile company. Including getting to the station, waiting for the train, getting to my appointment in uptown Manhattan, and returning home, my round trip travel time was approximately five hours, and the cost was about $70. All for a 40-minute meeting.

This company has licensed many other products from me, and we have a continuing relationship. I could perhaps have sent my prototype and presentation up by a package delivery service but that possibility frankly never entered my mind. I knew that if I made the presentation in person, my chances of selling it were light-years better than they would be doing it by mail. I was able to pitch my idea, answer questions, head off objections, and leave with a clear understanding of the status of my proposal and what would happen next. My contact, who loved the product, is having a new product meeting in four days and will call me when it's over. Before the end of the day, I had sent a fax (paper trail) confirming the results of our meeting and restating when I expected to hear from the company.

This is how you get the order. If you want to do business, you have to enter the marketplace, grab the prospect by the lapels, look that person in the eye, and *sell* him on your new idea. There are no substitutes for face-to-face selling so you might as well get ready for it. As Kit Carson said, "The cowards don't start and the weak die along the trail." I know you're not planning to be either.

If You Can See Them, You Can Sell Them

When you make up your prospect list, always keep geographical proximity in mind. Obviously, someone from Chicago has an advantage over someone from Fargo. But who said life is fair? If you do live in a small town where there aren't many companies, you should be aware of this when you're developing your ideas. Take an inventory of the companies you can reach and focus your thinking on products for them. It's a strategy that will definitely pay off.

Developing the actual prospect list is easy. For the camping utensil idea, a few visits to sporting goods stores and a search through catalogs and outdoor magazines should give you all the names you need. If that doesn't produce enough, looking through the *Thomas Register* at your local library should provide plenty more. This thick 19-volume set lists by category more companies than you could believe existed in one country. There are plenty of other reference books as well. Just ask the reference librarian.

Also, it would be worthwhile to ask the proprietor of a sporting goods store where and when the industry trade show is held. This is where all the sporting goods executives meet, and you could greatly expand access to your prospects by attending it. You can probably find a publication called *Directory of Conventions* in your local library. If you want to purchase it, the publisher's name and address can be found in the Appendix. This directory lists the dates and locations of virtually every trade show and convention in the country.

God Bless Trade Shows

Trade shows are heaven for me. I go to housewares shows, gift shows, toy shows, electronic shows, textile shows, and general merchandise shows. I've been to shows in England, Hong Kong, France, Taiwan, Ireland, Italy, Japan, and the Philippines. If I'm currently interested in developing or selling some giftware items, for instance, I'll go to the New York Gift Show, which is the largest in the world. Here I find literally thousands of companies and their executives. I browse, I talk, I make contacts, I survey the market, I make appointments, I find ideas, I make presentations.

If I have a product idea to present, on the first day or two I slowly walk through the entire exhibit hall, noting down the names and booth numbers of every firm that's a prospect for my new product idea. I put them in order, from the most likely to the least likely. On the first few days of a show, industry representatives are usually too busy with customers to talk to you. By the third day, however, they're happy to have the company. I visit as many of the more likely prospects that I can. I introduce myself to the president, or the representative in charge of new products, and make a date to see that person the next day or later that afternoon, depending on our mutual schedules. Whatever industry you're interested in undoubtedly has a trade show, and I'm sure you'll find it profitable to visit it.

When I first went into this business, I was nervous and would take my ideas for new products to small companies. I thought I'd be treated better and that they would welcome new ideas more readily than large ones. This was a big error and I wasted some terrific ideas. Yes, I sold them, but my royalties were a pittance compared with what they would have been with large companies.

The obvious reason is that little companies are little because they don't sell many products; and big companies are big because they sell a lot of products. And big companies need fresh ideas more than little guys because they have larger engines to stoke and more money to spend. And they'll treat you just fine. So don't be hesitant like me. Put the big companies at the top of your list. The little guys will always be there if you need them. Any successful salesperson will give you the same advice. If you were selling hammers, you wouldn't be calling on hardware stores if you could be spending the same time with the hammer buyer for Sears Roebuck.

DO YOU NEED AN AGENT? HOW TO FIND ONE; HOW TO GET ONE

Now that you've evaluated your list of prospects, this is a perfect time to say a few words about agents. Shall you contact these prospects yourself, or have someone do it for you? Benjamin Disraeli said, "It is well known what an agent is: He is a man who bamboozles one party and plunders the other." While agents are often the butt of jokes, in my experience they've been decent and helpful. Under certain circumstances, agents accomplished more for me than I could accomplish on my own, and I was happy to pay them their commission.

Who Are They?

My definition of an agent is simply someone who has access to decision makers, who will represent my interests to them in a professional manner, and whose remuneration is a percentage of the money earned by this effort. The key is that payment is in the form of commissions. Not advances, not fees, and not retainers. Invention marketing companies may claim that they'll act as your agent, but they're not true agents by this definition. They won't do a thing without payment in advance, and their claim of access to decision makers is laughable.

Where Do You Find Them?

Even if you're sold on the benefits of using an agent, there still exists the possibility that professional agents don't operate in your field. If what you've developed is an industrial product, you probably won't find an agent even if you want one. As a rule of thumb, where it's easier to see the prospective licensee, it's more difficult to find an agent. Since what agents are selling is a unique access to decision makers, they have to work in areas where that's a valuable commodity. For instance, if your new product is a children's game, you'll find it's quite difficult to meet the manufacturers because everybody's trying to sell them games. Agents exist in this field and, if you can get one, it would probably be worthwhile.

Do You Need Each Other?

You may feel you need an agent, but chances are the agent won't feel a comparable need for you. Most licensing agents I know turn down many more clients than they accept. If they don't think your product has merit, which is usually the case, they'll politely tell you so. By being selective, their value (and their access) to the decision makers is enhanced. The executive at a game company, for example, will see a professional licensing agent because it is an efficient use of his time. The agent is going to present a prescreened, small selection of games, each of which is worth consideration. The manufacturer doesn't know your work, so without a connection, it would be extremely difficult to get your own appointment.

On the other hand, if your invention is a terrific new attachment for an automatic metal spinning machine, the manufacturer will probably tell you to come right over because not too many people have terrific new ideas for metal spinning machines. Agents usually don't exist in these industries, but if they did, you wouldn't need them. As a rule, if you can get to the decision maker yourself, don't use an agent. You'll do a better job because you know more about your product. If you can't get to the decision maker, I suggest you make an agent out of anyone who can.

If you do try to get an agent and are turned down, don't be discouraged or take it personally. All agents can tell you horror tales of products they rejected that someone else later turned into blockbusters. The interesting thing about this business is that *nobody* knows for sure what constitutes a winning product. Successful people simply happen to guess right more often than they guess wrong.

If you want to find out if agents exist in your field, you can do this by checking in your industry's "who makes it" directory. This is usually published yearly by that particular industry's leading magazines. For details, ask for the Standard Rate and Data Service at your local library.

What Do They Want from You?

If you decide to use a licensing agent, and if you can find one, and if the agent agrees to represent you, you'll have to sign a contract. I've seen some that are one page and some that are six or more pages, but they all essentially have the same few basic points:

1. Commission arrangement.
2. Exclusivity:
    A. By area.
    B. By time.
3. Method of payment.
4. Cancellation procedure and rights.

Commission arrangements are so capricious that it's difficult to offer advice. Agents in some fields charge 10 percent. In other fields, they charge up to 50 percent. There's no logic to the percentage, and only you can decide if it's worth it. The only comforting thought is that, regardless of the percentage, they don't get any money unless they license your product. Usually, the more input they make, the higher the commission they demand. Agents are quite perceptive and usually know what will sell. If they whip your product idea into more salable shape, and if they refashion your presentation to make it more professional, how can you argue if they ask for 25, or 35, or even 40 percent? If they turn it into a million-dollar licensing deal, could you live on a 65 percent cut?

Every legitimate licensing company will expect to represent you on an exclusive basis. Their territory is often the world. Usually, they want this exclusivity for a year or two; then they automatically renew it year to year thereafter unless either party cancels. This means that regardless of when or where in the world your product is sold, they get their percentage. If you happen to mention your product idea to a woman standing in front of you in a supermarket line in Bucharest, and if she owns a company that happens to be looking for exactly that product, and if you license it to her, your agent in New York still gets the same commission.

In your agreement, you'll give the agent the authority to negotiate on your behalf. If your product is licensed, the royalty check goes to your agent. After the check has been deposited and has cleared, the agent will send you his or her own check, from which the commission has been deducted. Naturally, the agent will also send along the sales reports from the licensee.

How Do You and Your Agent Part Friends?

Your agent is required to keep you informed as to what companies have been called on and the results of the call. If you decide to fire the agent, he or she is still entitled to any royalties that may be earned from any of these companies, even if it happens years later.

Client–agent relations in most fields are volatile and often don't last long. The client thinks the agent isn't looking after his interests, and the agent thinks the account is a waste of time. This is the nature of these relationships so it's not such a tragedy if you let your agent go at the end of the contract. Besides, an agent who hasn't sold your product by then, will have no cause to object. Clients are so easy to find (particularly ones that generate no money) that the agent will hardly know you're gone. Just keep your parting on a professional level. Business is business. Besides, you may need that agent again someday.

Use Special Agents Whenever You Can: It's the American Way

I've acted as an agent myself on several occasions. Why not? I can professionally represent the interests of the client and I have access to certain decision makers. My arrangements are situational. I tell the client (usually a friend or professional acquaintance) which companies I intend to show the idea to.

If I'm successful in getting it licensed, fine. If I'm not, we each go our own way with no harm done. There are lots of people like me around, and you should use us. Since what we're selling is access to decision makers, you can make an agent of anyone who has it. It can be a friend, an in-law, your attorney, or your accountant. Ask around. Don't be shy. It's just another form of good old fashioned networking. I spend a great deal of time in Asia, working on products for clients. There, everybody's second occupation is being an agent. Introductions are bought and sold all the time. They provide the grease that turns the wheels of commerce. It's the same in Washington. Arranging access to decision makers has made millionaires out of more than one former congressman or general.

GETTING THE APPOINTMENT: THE MAGIC TWO-MINUTE TELEPHONE CONVERSATION

Depending on your disposition, we're now at the point you've been waiting for or dreading. This is where the selling begins. In just the briefest of telephone calls you have to convince some tough, high-powered executive to make time to see you. Will he or she laugh? Slam the phone down? Tell you to go fly a kite?

You can relax. In most industries, getting an appointment is easy. You just need to stretch the truth a little and have a little nerve. After you do it once, it's fun. Just follow these simple, foolproof instructions:

Four Things to Remember When You Call for an Appointment

1. *You Are Not an Amateur!* Companies are disinclined to deal with nonprofessionals. Rarely do amateurs have

anything worth showing, and amateurs are much more wary than professionals about having their ideas stolen. Having learned from experience, companies don't want to be sued by trigger-happy neophytes who think that everybody who looks at them intently is out to steal their ideas. Professionals behave more rationally, often have more reasoned proposals, and are therefore automatically made welcome.

So consider yourself at war. And the first casualty of war is the truth. You are *not* going to call the Green Velvet Mower Company and announce that you're actually a computer programmer by trade, but you have a cute idea for a lawn mower. By innuendo, you're going to present yourself as a successful professional. I'll show you in a moment what I mean.

2. *Go for the President.* You should usually try to reach the president of the company. You can't always do it, but you'll be successful more often than you think. If you can't get to the president, try for the number two person. If you're calling a giant company such as Johnson & Johnson, you'll certainly not get through to the president, and you probably wouldn't want him anyway. But there is someone in charge of the division you're interested in, and that's the person you want to talk to.

    Whatever happens, don't put yourself into the hands of some third-level assistant who promises to show your presentation to the boss (who is away on vacation right now). Nothing good can come from such a contact.

    Decision makers are deceptively accessible. Call one day and get the name. Call the next day and just tell the operator to connect you to good old Bill Duffy. It's really quite simple.

3. *Keep It Brief.* When you get Bill Duffy on the phone, keep your conversation as short as possible without being rude. Remember that all you're calling for is an appointment. When you get it, say thank you and hang

**Be as Brief as Possible
When You Call for an Appointment**

up. If you wind up chatting with Duffy on the telephone, you're going to say too much and your appointment's may get canceled right before your eyes.

Good old Bill is going to find out that you're actually a computer programmer and that you've never done this before; worst of all, you're going to say too much about your idea. He'll decide the meeting isn't really necessary and will request that you just send some information to look over before getting back to you. As someone named Olin Miller once said, "When a person says he'll let you know—you know."

Consider yourself a commando. Understand your mission (an appointment), make the raid (the call), and get out as soon as your mission's accomplished. If you hang around to see your handiwork, you're a goner.

4. *Niceness Pays.* Always be pleasant and friendly to switchboard operators, secretaries, and aides. They're often the keys to executive access. If you come across on the phone as a friendly person, they'll be inclined to help. If you're nasty, they may find a way to get even.

It often happens that you'll be in some executive's office, showing her a new product concept, and she'll invite her secretary in. "Shirley," she says, "you just bought a new car. What do you think of this doo-hickey?" For your sake, I hope you were nice to Shirley.

Here the script for a short, one-act play that I've acted in dozens and dozens of times. It's called *The Appointment:*

The Cast:

HELEN FURY
switchboard operator

MAX DUBOIS
President, Global
Amalgamated Things, Ltd.

DONNA MADONNA
Dubois' secretary

HECTOR GREENBOTTOM
executive vice president

BUSTER BALDWIN
Hector Greenbottom's
assistant

THOMAS ALVA REDDISON
Handsome, young inventor

Fury: Hello Global. Can you hold? (*Good. A busy switchboard operator doesn't have time for questions.*)

Fury: Hello. Sorry to keep you waiting.

Reddison: That's OK. Let me have Max Dubois please. (*Reddison will have called a few days earlier to get the president's name. The way he's made the request implies he and Dubois are old friends. If Ms. Fury asks any questions, Reddison just says he has something for Dubois and asks again to be put through.*)

Fury: Ringing . . .

Madonna: Hello. Mr. Dubois' office.

Reddison: Hi. My name's Tom Reddison. We design products for companies and we just created something that I know Max will want. So if you could put me through I'd appreciate it. (*Warm, friendly voice. If Reddison were an insurance person, he*

> *would need to use a different approach, but since Dubois is going to be curious, the direct approach is best. Note Reddison says "we," never "I."*

Madonna: . . . moment.

Dubois: Dubois here.

Reddison: Hi Mr. Dubois. Thanks for taking my call. I know you're busy, so I'll be brief. We design new products for companies and we've hit upon something that I think can be very special for Global Amalgamated. If I could have a few minutes to show it to you, I promise you won't be disappointed. *(This is a perfect 15-second presentation. Reddison has thanked Dubois, flattered him by acknowledging how busy he is, stated the purpose of the call, piqued his interest, and asked for an appointment).* The use of "we" suggests one company contacting another.

At this point, Dubois will say one of three things:

1. OK: When do you want to come in?
2. Sounds interesting. What have you got?
3. Oh, you want Hector Greenbottom. He handles all the new products.

If Dubois' answer is Number 1 (When do you want to come in?), Reddison make the appointment and hangs up promptly, after giving the secretary his telephone number in case Dubois has to cancel. If nobody knew how to reach Reddison, he might drive from Pittsburgh to Cleveland only to find that Dubois was out sick. It happens.

If Dubois' answer is Number 2 (What have you got?) Reddison answers as follows:

Reddison: I really can't do it justice by trying to describe it over the telephone, but when you see the drawings (or model), I know you'll be excited. It fits with what you're doing and I promise I won't be wasting your time. *(Dubois agrees to the appointment.)*

If Dubois' answer is Number 3 (Oh, you want Hector Greenbottom), Reddison asks to be switched.

Baldwin: Mr. Greenbottom's office. *(Baldwin is a screener. He's authorized to say no, but he can't say yes. Avoid him at all costs. Baldwin learned a long time ago that you can get into trouble by saying yes, but you almost never get into trouble by saying no.)*

Reddison: Hi. My name's Tom Reddison. We create new products for companies and we've recently developed something for Global that Max wanted us to show to Mr. Greenbottom. So if you could put me through, I'd appreciate it. *(Reddison speaks to Greenbottom, repeats his pitch, fends off a request to describe the product, and makes the appointment.)*

Except for the waiting time, this whole exercise should only take two or three minutes, and you almost certainly will get an appointment. Never, ever describe your idea on the telephone. It takes the mystery out of your visit, and you run the risk that the person on the phone will lose interest. If you simply explain that a telephone description won't do it justice, and that the person is really going to like the product, you'll almost always get the appointment. Sometimes, out of curiosity, the person will say something like "OK, but can't you just give me a hint?" Just give a warm chuckle and offer reassurance that your visit will not be disappointing. I've almost never been denied an appointment once I had the right party on the telephone. Every company executive wants to learn about a new idea that may benefit the company. These people didn't get where they are by being foolish. They just want to be sure they won't waste time with some amateur who doesn't know anything about the business.

Making a Mail Solicitation That's Slightly Better than Nothing

Even if it's not possible for you to make a personal sales visit, and if you therefore plan to mail the material, you should still call first. Your telephone conversation will be similar to the one we just reviewed, up to the point where you ask for an appointment. Instead, you'll tell Mr. Dubois that you have this terrific idea and you'd like to send him some information. Find a reason to chat with him for a moment or two so he'll remember you when your material arrives. Your covering letter can then remind Mr. Dubois of your telephone conversation, thank him for his courtesy, and state the enclosed material is being sent at his suggestion. It's not as good as a personal visit, but it's much better than an unsolicited mailing.

And while we're on the subject of material, *never* send your original! With the best intentions, material may get lost, or thrown out, or you may have to wait months to have it returned. In the meantime, you're dead in the water. For color work, find a Canon copier. The color reproduction will be almost as good as the original. And send the material to Mr. Dubois via an overnight delivery service or the Post Office's priority mail service. Certainly, it costs a few dollars more, but it makes your presentation special.

If you have ever bought mutual funds, your name was probably sold to brokerage houses, and suddenly you were inundated with calls from people you didn't know who wanted to sell you stocks. I don't know about you, but for me it's out of the question to make investments with strangers like this. They may be fine, legitimate people, but I turn a deaf ear.

I suspect that unsolicited new product offerings received in the mail are treated with the same hostile response. To present a new concept in that fashion is so belittling to the idea that the recipient has mentally said no before even finishing reading the letter. If the recipient can connect your name with a previous telephone conversation, and if your letter addresses the executive by name and says that the material is enclosed in response to a request, it at least lessens the "Who is the guy?" problem.

Confessions of a Habitual Failure

Personally, I've never ever made a successful new product submission by mail to a company that didn't already know me. Even though I've always called the prospect first and even though I've always chatted with the prospect on the telephone, and even though I've always sent a first-class presentation, I have never been able to close a sale. I have tried *many* times, but the caliber of my ideas must be such that I'm unable to get people excited with a letter. If pitching your product by letter is the only way you can do it, I hope you have better luck.

On the other hand, the good news is that once you've sold one product to a company, they're far more inclined to buy a second and third from you regardless of how you transmit it to them. If the company knows you and trusts you, you'll find that the fax is the best invention of the twentieth century.

Even Grown-Ups Have Wish Lists

In the toy industry, where every year means a new battle in the marketplace, toy companies cater to established toy developers. It's fair to say that many smaller companies owe their very existence to independent product developers. They invite them to private showings of their line, they hold cocktail parties for them, and most importantly, they provide "wish lists." These lists outline the areas in which the company is looking for toys for the following year, such as "We

**If You Have What a Company Is Looking for, You Can Just
about Tie a Sketch to a Brick and Throw It through the
President's Window**

need craft items, outdoor water toys and electronic games."
If you have something on the list, you can tie a sketch to a
brick and throw it through the president's window. The company will still be happy to buy it from you.

If the primary reason to conduct your business in person is
that it greatly improves your chances of success, the secondary reason is that you get to know the company and the
kind of products they're looking for. And they get to know
you. You'll never acquire this kind of knowledge, or establish
this kind of relationship, through the mail. When you know
what the company wants, it helps to focus your thinking for
future products. They supply the problem, you supply the solution. Before you know it, a valuable alliance has formed.

When you proceed to dream up a new product idea, it helps
a great deal if you already have a company in mind to sell it
to. You can create your first idea in a vacuum, but if you

intend to do it over and over, it facilitates matters greatly to have a target company in mind. Once you've licensed your first product to a company, you'll probably be able to continue doing it. You can't develop profitable relationships through the mail, so the sooner you start phoning for appointments, the better.

THE CONCEPT OF THE NONDISCLOSURE FORM. DO YOU SIGN THEIRS OR DO THEY SIGN YOURS? AND DOES IT MATTER?

For the sake of our discussion, let's assume that the product you've created is an attachment for an automatic lathe. Manufacturers of industrial equipment don't get that many calls from people who have great product ideas for them, so your telephone call will almost exactly follow our script and you'll be invited to come right over.

On the other hand, if you've developed something like a new toy or a new kitchen gadget, you may run into a different reception. Large, high-profile consumer goods companies have people contacting them *all the time* with new product ideas. These companies devour new products at great speed and in big gulps, so they're always looking for something new and exciting. If you have next year's hot toy or a new automatic bread maker, they definitely want to hear from you. However, as the old saying goes, you have to kiss a lot of frogs before you meet a prince. The truth of the matter is that most new product submissions aren't worth the powder to blow them up. The ideas are stale, half-formed, or half-baked, or they have no relevancy to the company's business. Almost all of them are a waste of a company's time.

To make matters worse, many amateurs who submit these concepts have an unrealistic estimate of their idea's worth as well as a possessiveness about it that borders on paranoia. And even if the product submitted does have merit, there's still the possibility that the company is already working on it. The company then runs the risk that the inventor will cry foul and go running to an attorney. The defense that some large companies use is a Product Submission Form. The company says, "Hey, we'd *love* to see your new product idea, and we bet it's terrific! One little thing though; please sign this form so we know that you understand and accept the way we operate."

Read It and Weep

1. The company says to please not send your idea until you've given it all the legal protection you can. Because that's the only protection you'll have. Patent it if you can, or at least copyright it. If you don't do either, proceed at your own risk. The company assumes no responsibility.

2. You are making the submission on your own initiative and by your own free will. Nothing has been promised to you. Further, you understand that it's possible the company may already be working on the same or a similar idea, which makes your submission redundant.

3. You understand and agree that:

    A. The company does not agree to keep your idea confidential.

    B. The company does not promise to return your materials.

    C. The company doesn't promise to pay you anything for your idea.

    The only recourse you have is whatever protection is provided by your patent or copyright. If your idea doesn't have either, you have no protection whatsoever.

And have a nice day.

The Mead Corporation is an enlightened company, anxious to see whatever new ideas you might wish to show the company. Nevertheless, if you make contact, you'll receive the following form letter from their legal department:

Dear _____:

Mead is always receptive to new ideas and designs, as can be seen from the enclosed write-up "Mead Welcomes Ideas," which also outlines the conditions under which new ideas and designs will be evaluated. If you agree with the conditions as set forth in the write-up, please sign and return the form as indicated, together with the idea or design you would like Mead to evaluate, to my attention at the above address.

Your idea or design will then be evaluated and, thereafter, we will relay to you the results of the evaluation.

Thank you for considering Mead in this matter. We look forward to hearing you in the near future.

Very truly yours,

Included with the letter is the following:

Mead Welcomes New Ideas

The Mead Corporation welcomes ideas and designs and will evaluate outside submissions if the idea or design relates to our business.

Of course, we are not interested in ideas or designs that we may already know about, or that are in the public domain. We have many projects on which we are now working, and many inventions of our own which we have not yet put into operation.

To protect you, as well as ourselves, we must follow a definite procedure in handling such ideas and designs.

What Subjects Are Acceptable

Your idea should encompass a new or improved process, machine, product, composition of matter, or design relative to some phase of Mead's business. In general, Mead's business interests include paper and related products, paperboard and related products, metals and minerals, interior furnishings, consumer and educational products, pulp and forest products and information technology.

Design Submissions

Frequently, designs and ideas for the use of certain designs are submitted to Mead. These designs are often in the form of drawings, sketches, photographs or the like. You should note that mere general suggestions are treated by the law as abstract ideas and only the specific embodiments or expressions are subject to protection by design patents or copyrights. Therefore, you must keep in mind that in submitting your design to Mead for evaluation, you agree that your submission is limited to the particular design(s) submitted and does not encompass whatever marketing or other generic concept might be associated with such design(s). By the way of example, if you submit a photograph of a scenic river and suggest its use on notebook covers, your submission is limited to the particular representation appearing in the photograph you submit, and would not extend to other natural scenes, whether or not such scenes include scenic rivers.

Your Protection

The United States patent system protects inventors against unauthorized use of their inventions and the United States copyright system affords protection to authors against copying of their work. Therefore, for the protection of both you and Mead, you must understand that, in submitting and thus disclosing an idea or design to us, you rely upon your patent or copyright rights, present or future, for your protection against unauthorized use of your invention or design. You should fully protect your idea or design to your own satisfaction before submitting it for our consideration. You should bear in mind that in submitting your idea to Mead under a non-confidential relationship, you may well be jeopardizing or forfeiting patent rights in certain foreign countries in which you have not yet filed patent applications.

How to Submit Your Idea

We prefer that you either apply for or obtain a patent or copyright your idea or design before sending it to us.

When this proves impossible, make a written record of your idea or design in duplicate. Sign and date both copies and have one or more persons to whom you have explained your idea or design sign and date them, too. One of the copies can then be submitted to us, in accordance with the conditions outlined herein. Keep the other copy. While such a written record does not, of itself, give patent or copyright protection, it would be of use in proving priority of invention, should the need arise. Further, this provides a record of what you disclose to us.

Consideration of Disclosures

Mead will not accept or examine written descriptions of idea or designs under a confidential relationship. Although we have no intention of publicizing an idea or design which may be sent to us, we cannot guarantee that it will be held in secrecy.

In an idea or design is sent to us, it must be the free act of the inventor and it must be in concrete form for our records. This record will be on hand later if any question should arise as to the nature of the idea or design.

If your idea or design is novel and possibly patentable or copyrightable and could be used by Mead, we may want to negotiate with you about acquiring rights therein.

How Ideas Should Be Sent

When you wish to submit an idea or design to us, attach it to the form on page 3 completed in full and signed. Do not disclose your idea or design to any of our sales people or other employees, but send it directly to the address given on the form.

What Happens after an Idea Is Submitted

When we receive the completed form and your written idea or design, we will examine the form and subject matter. Any written idea or design which is not attached to a completed and signed form, or does not deal with the subject matter previously listed, will be returned to you.

If your idea or design is properly submitted and the subject matter is within our range of interest, we will review it and give you our evaluation of it.

And here, in conclusion, are the conditions you must agree to before sending your new product concept to Mead Corporation:

Conditions of Submission

1. All submissions or disclosures of ideas and designs are voluntary on the part of the submitter. No confidential relationship is to be established or implied from consideration of the submitted material.

2. With respect to unpatentable or uncopyrightable ideas and designs Mead will consider them only with the understanding that the use to be made of such ideas and designs and the compensation, if any, to be paid for them are matters resting solely in the discretion of the company.

3. With respect to patentable or copyrightable idea and designs, including those covered by patents, pending patent applications and registered or unregistered copyrights, Mead will consider them only with the understanding that the submitter agrees to rely for his protection wholly on such rights as he may have under the patent and copyright laws of the United States. With respect to ideas and designs included in this subsection, Mead may want to negotiate with the submitter about acquiring rights therein.

4. It is understood that idea and design submissions or disclosures are limited to the specific embodiment or expression submitted and do not extend to any marketing concept or other generic concept which may be associated with said specific embodiment or expression.

5. The foregoing conditions may not be modified or waived.*

As foreboding as these documents may sound, the conditions are not unreasonable from the corporation's point of view. After all, they didn't come to you, you came to them. The bright side is that companies like Mead would *never* steal your idea, and if what you show them has merit, they'll be pleased to

---

*"Mead Welcomes New Ideas" and "Conditions of Submission," are published by the Mead Corporation. Used with permission.

negotiate with you to get it. So don't worry about it. Just sign on the dotted line.

If I call a new company for an appointment, and if the person I'm planning to see tells me that the company has a nondisclosure form, I tell him fine, just fax it to me. I sign the form and fax it right back, sometimes while we're both still on the telephone. Rarely do I bother to read it because I already know what it says. I know my rights, and I know I'm not the person the company's trying to protect itself from. It may be rash for me to suggest that you sign so easily, but you're really not giving away any legitimate rights and these companies won't look at your idea unless you comply. They must protect themselves from cranks, and I know that description doesn't apply to you.

Some attorneys and well-meaning friends may suggest that you have your own nondisclosure form, which you should get the company to sign before telling them about your idea. The company would promise to keep your information strictly confidential, they would promise to return your materials as soon as you requested them, and if no deal was made, the company would promise not to commercially profit by whatever they learned from you. These are all totally reasonable requests, except that companies don't sign these things. You'll only spend your money needlessly and delay the process. You can't teach a pig to sing. You waste your time and you annoy the pig.

We have our appointment, we've signed the nondisclosure form, and our presentation is as crisp and professional looking as it could be. Now we move on to my favorite part of the CRASH program. We're ready to meet eyeball to eyeball with the person who's going to pay a fortune for our new product idea.

5

MEETING WITH
THE PROSPECT

How to Make a
Successful Sales Pitch

*I don't like money, but
it quiets my nerves.*

—Joe Louis

I'm one of the lucky people of the world because I love the
work I do. I wear jeans almost every day, I shave about
twice a week, and while everyone else is rushing to work, I'm
enjoying my second cup of coffee. I work at home, at my own
pace, and every month the royalty checks get delivered in the
mail.

"Do what you like, do it the best you can, and the money will
follow." I've heard that advice offered countless times over
the years, usually by someone older to someone younger. It
didn't make sense to me when I was a young man, just as it
probably doesn't make sense to young people today. Nevertheless, I'm living proof that it works. Until middle age,
everything I did was for the purpose of making money.

When bankruptcy caused me to change careers, I decided to just do what I like, and to do it the very best way I knew how. And, sure enough, the money did follow.

And the part of work that I like the most is taking my latest product idea under my arm and going out to sell it. It's a special event because I put on a jacket and tie and I get to go someplace. And what could be more rewarding than getting someone excited by the product of your own creativity? It's the Rolls Royce of selling.

NO CALL IS A WASTED CALL

I don't make a sale on every call, not by a long shot, but each call is valuable and I'm always glad I made it. If my product isn't right for the company I'm calling on, an executive there will often direct me to the company it *is* right for. "Go see Billy Kramer over at Kramer's Thingarama. This should be perfect for him. And be sure to tell him I sent you over!" And even if company representatives don't like my idea, they'll often offer suggestions that help improve it. And sometimes they point out fatal flaws in my idea. When that happens, I simply file the design away and move on to the next project. So no call is wasted and, if nothing else, I may have made a contact for my next idea.

I approach each call with the confidence that my prospects are going to love what I show them. Dale Carnegie called it the *Power of Positive Thinking*. I don't know why it works, but it does. It's an aura of success that all good salespeople have, and they don't even have the personal satisfaction of selling their own creation. Very few people can create an original, commercial idea, so you should carry yourself into the meeting with great pride. It'll reflect in your voice and in your actions and, most important, in the product you're presenting. Your accomplishment commands respect, and in most instances, you'll get it.

A SALESPERSON'S WORST NIGHTMARE: PART I

I recently had an appointment with a company president whom I had never met before. I showed up for my appointment exactly on time, as is my habit, and was kept waiting in a tiny, windowless, reception room for about 40 minutes. Finally I was ushered into the great woman's office. I wasn't greeted with an apology or even a "hello." I wasn't even offered a seat. Instead, as I entered, I was abruptly informed that she was quite busy and could only give me 10 minutes. I should also mention that she knew I had driven more than two hours to get to her office.

I realized that there was no hope in saving the situation so I told her to forget it. I told her politely but firmly that what I had was worth more than 10 minutes and perhaps one day I'd come back and we could start over. With that, I simply turned and left. I must confess that the stunned silence was music to my ears.

Over the next several weeks she had her secretary call me on three different occasions to ask if I was ready to reschedule the appointment and each time I replied that I was not. She obviously realized that she might have let something of value slip through her fingers. Just between us, it was actually not such a sensational product—I suspect her imagination did more for it than I could have ever done. I never did go back and eventually sold the product to her competitor. To this day, she doesn't know what it is, nor does she know what subsequent products I might have shown her if she had made me feel more welcome. It's not a matter of being cocky. I simply felt that I was prepared to offer her something of value and was therefore entitled to a degree of courtesy. When you're a product developer you can afford to do this. There are so few of us, and so many companies that need what we're selling.

A SALESPERSON'S WORST NIGHTMARE: PART II

As a very young man, I had a job as a salesperson on the road. On my first day, on my very first call, I had an experience that will stay with me forever. My appointment was with a supermarket buyer, and sitting in the waiting room I was as nervous as any neophyte would be. Finally my turn came, and I was directed to his office. It was a typical buyer's office. Small, airless, piled high with papers and samples. Old wooden furniture. Like visiting a cheap detective. And there he sat, waiting for me. Hooded eyes, open collar. No smile, no greeting. I said hello, he nodded. As soon as I was seated, he reached over, cranked an egg timer, and said "OK kid, you've got three minutes."

To my credit, I didn't pass out. The ticking of the timer was like Big Ben on speed, each bong bringing me closer to my doom. Flustered, embarrassed, and rattled, I broke all records speeding through my presentation (I must have done it in less than a minute), plunked down my catalog sheets, mumbled my thanks, and stumbled out of the office.

I'd like to tell you that he actually placed an order and that we ultimately became the best of friends. But he didn't and we didn't. What I did get out of the experience, however, was much more valuable. I vowed never again to allow myself to be treated this way by a buyer, and it never did happen again. That is, not until 30 years later when a company president gave me 10 minutes to tell my story. From 3 minutes to 10 minutes is not very much progress, when you allow for inflation.

Actually, little episodes like these are rarities. What's more typical is to be treated with hospitality and consideration by the people you call on. They are *hoping* that you're going to show them something special, so they'll greet you in an anticipatory mood. Executives love to see interesting new products. It's the lifeblood of their business. Other salespeople would be thrilled to have their prospects greet them in this frame of mind.

ESTABLISHING YOUR CREDENTIALS

The natural way to start any meeting is to tell something about yourself and why you're taking up this busy person's time. People have a preconceived image of an inventor that is not always flattering. The adjective "crackpot" immediately leaps to mind and makes licensees a little uneasy. Let them see what a nice, bright regular type person you are, and that you know what you're talking about. It'll put your prospects at ease and make them more receptive to your presentation.

When I call for an appointment, I never describe myself as an inventor since it tends to be off-putting. I call myself a product developer, which has a more businesslike tone. I want to be viewed as a businessperson whose business it is to sell profit-making ideas.

Allowing for obvious differences, male and female executives dress the same in similar circumstances. A female marketing executive for a Fortune 500 company projects the same sartorial image as her male counterpart. Therefore, either way, I'm able to dress similarly and can present myself as someone who fits into the environment. As best I can, I become like my prospect in dress and speech so that he or she will be more mentally prepared to hear my story. The signing of a license is usually the beginning of a relationship, so if you can give clues that it will be a pleasant one, you're that much ahead of the game.

Let's say you're sitting with Mr. Stewart Bunyon, President of the Universal Camping Equipment Company, preparing to show him your new idea for biodegradable, disposable eating utensils. You're obviously going to gloss over the fact that you're a computer programmer by profession. But you're going to stress that you're a veteran camper of 18 years, that you've camped out in 27 states and three provinces in Canada, and that you've been using Ajax Camping Equipment since way back when your dad used to take you out. Mr. Bunyon is obviously a camper himself and perhaps has visited some of the same camps. You will have established a foundation to build your relationship. Whatever your credentials are, this is the time to establish them. It's your audiovisual business card.

IT'S YOUR PITCH, SO PUT SOMETHING ON THE BALL

Although you're not exactly selling cemetery lots, you're a salesperson now, and any salesperson's first job is to establish rapport with his customer and earn some respect. You're going to want Mr. Bunyon ("Call me 'Stu'") to accept some of what you're about to say on blind faith, so it's important that he like and trust you. You had good background reasons for inventing *this* product and showing it to *this* company, and that information should be on the table from the very beginning. It is important for Stu to recognize your knowledge about camping because it adds legitimacy to your product idea.

I've met a number of "typical" inventors over the years and find many are so wrapped up in the *process* of inventing that it becomes an end in itself. Most inventors are, first and foremost, problem solvers. The joy to them is in finding the solution to the problem, and the money part is a secondary nuisance. The actual act of inventing is what keeps them going, and they're reluctant to invest time in selling their products. That may explain why such a large percentage of patented products are never commercialized. Many inventors hate the idea of going out to peddle their wares; they feel that should be somebody else's job.

If that was your attitude before reading this book, you'd better lose it now. If you can't go out and make an enthusiastic sales presentation for your own idea, who can? Seeing the commercial version of your product in a beautiful box on a retail shelf can also reflect the joy of creativity. And there is true pleasure in knowing that every time somebody buys one of your products, anywhere in the world, you're being paid for it. If you want to succeed, you must remember that you're not in the invention business. You're in the profit business. Anyone can get a good idea. Almost everybody does from time to time. What separates the professionals from the amateurs (and what makes some product developers very rich) is turning a dream into a commercial reality. Nothing wonderful is going to happen to you or your idea until you go out and sell it. And this is the time to begin.

THE TRUTH WILL SET YOU FREE

Now that you're about to swing into your presentation, you must be totally honest in your claims and representations. I know I encouraged you to gloss the truth a bit to get the appointment, but that was then and this is now. Righteousness has nothing to do with it; honesty is simply a matter of good business sense. So much of what the customer thinks of your idea has to do with what he or she thinks of you that only a fool would jeopardize the relationship with false statements. If there's any interest in your product, and if you make any untruthful or exaggerated claims, I promise you'll ultimately be found out. When that happens, it may be an extremely expensive lesson.

SAY HELLO TO THE DIRECTOR
OF RESEARCH

"Frank, do you have a few minutes? I've got a guy in my office with a new product idea you oughta take a look at." Frank, it turns out, is the company's research and development director and, you must assume, commands Stu's respect. If you're automatically suspicious that Frank could be a deal-breaker, your instincts may be correct. A research director called into a boss's office to give an opinion about a new product idea from an outsider is not inclined to be your ally. It goes with the territory. Here's what I mean.

The Dreaded NIH Disease

I know a woman who's in charge of product research for a giftware company in Long Island, New York. For years I would bring her new product ideas, and for years she turned me down. She's a nice person and was unfailingly polite and interested when I made my presentations. But, although she'd always ask that I leave my drawings and prototypes for further study, the ultimate answer would always be the same, "Sorry, but we decided it's too expensive (or too cheap, or too big, or too small)."

I knew the products I presented were as good as or better than what her company was selling, and giftware companies always need new products, so I was baffled by my repeated failure. One day, out of the blue, I finally realized the problem. The poor woman was afflicted with the dreaded NIH disease!

"Not Invented Here" is a widespread sickness that rarely affects company presidents and marketing people, but often strikes research directors, engineers, and product managers. It's the tendency to believe that any product presented by an outsider can't possibly be as good as those developed internally. It's an ego-driven illness that can sometimes be contained by massive doses of compliments and outward manifestations of respect. Confrontational treatment usually results in severe relapses.

So with this in mind, you must be prepared to handle Frank with the assumption that he's similarly afflicted. The trick is to make him look good, without making yourself look bad. Here's a snippet of the kind of conversation that you must avoid:

Stu: So what do you think we can get for it?

You: I think $10.00 seems just about right because Consolidated sells their utensil set for $7.95 and ours has all these extra features . . .

Frank: So whatta you think it'll cost to produce?

You: I've looked at that very closely, and it shouldn't cost more than about $3.00, depending on whether you go with plastic or wood.

A smile creeps across Frank's face because now you're in big trouble. He can see that you didn't do your homework. You should know that, in the camping business, a manufacturer needs at least a five-time multiple from cost to retail to make a profit. So if the cost to produce the item is $3.00, the company needs a retail of at least $15.00. And you've already said the optimum retail is $10.00. So now what? Were you correct at either end, or were you guessing? Do you *really* know that $10.00 is the best retail? Are you *really* sure about the cost figures? You get the idea.

The question of manufacturing costs versus selling price comes up at virtually every meeting, and I always duck it if I can. Let's rerun the scene:

Stu: So what do you think we can get for it?

You: Well, you and Frank know pricing strategy far better than I do, but it's certainly worth more than Consolidated's set. I think consumers will gladly pay a bit more for our version. What do you think the right retail should be? Obviously (turning to Frank) you know more about marketing than I do.

Frank: OK, first tell me what you think it'll cost to produce.

You: I have a rough cost breakdown here (*shows figures*), but with your company's production skills, I know you'll do much better. The important thing is, even using my figures, you can see that there's ample room for profits. To be perfectly honest, Frank, I trust your judgment on this better than mine. It's obvious that you know what you're doing.

I then sit back and let Stu and Frank work it out between them. They do it all the time, and after a little give and take, they quickly come to a resolution and the product has now become theirs. I don't look bad by saying I don't know, and I've shown respect for Frank's ability. I'll keep the conversation in this tone, and hopefully, will have Frank on my side before the meeting is over. Even if I really did have an opinion of the best retail and even if I did know the precise production costs, I would rather involve the prospect if I can. It conditions the person to start thinking of the product as belonging to the company, not to me. And that, after all, is the whole purpose of this exercise.

FIVE SIMPLE TIPS, ALL WORTH REPEATING

Your written proposal will pretty much dictate the agenda of the meeting, so here are a few points to remember as you get started:

1. Whatever you do, don't read your presentation. Your customer will start to doze off, and your credibility will fly out the window.

2. Don't give out a copy of your written presentation until you have finished your oral presentation. It will encourage your customer to read a page or two ahead of you instead of listening to you.

3. Move along at a brisk pace. Your audience of one (or several) catches on quickly and if you drag things out, their minds will start to wander.

4. Don't unveil your prototype until the proper time. And when you do bring it out, place it in your prospect's

Rule #1: Never Read Your Presentation

hands, implying that it's not yours anymore. It's the customer's.

5. If you need extension cords or batteries for a projector or recorder, bring them with you and have everything set up before you begin.

These basic rules will help you give a superior presentation. Many of your customers have spent so much of their lives in worthless meetings that they appreciate the occasional good ones. It will reflect well on you and your new product.

GATHER AROUND, BOYS AND GIRLS: IT'S STORY TIME

When I proceed with my presentation, I do it as if I were telling a story to a child. Everyone, no matter how mature or sophisticated, likes a good story with a happy ending. Maybe I don't actually start with "Once upon a time," but the implication is there. Top salespeople will tell you that one of the most effective ways to make a point is to tell a personal story that has a bearing on it. Have you ever met anyone who wouldn't pause to hear a good story? My stories all have to do with how silly old me just happened to dream up this terrific new product that brought us together. Shucks, anyone could do it:

> One day, I stopped to watch those guys putting up the new IBM building down on Spruce Street when, out of the corner of my eye, I happened to notice . . .

> I promised my wife I'd pick up a new hair dryer, so I was in Kmart over near the Market Village Mall and I wandered over to the automotive department and was amazed to see . . .

> I popped into the new computer store they just opened next to Ellworth Drugs on Pine Street when I saw this big crowd gathered around a display. I went over to check it out and couldn't help laughing when I found . . .

If I can get my prospects to agree that a problem actually exists in the first place, I have a good chance of convincing them that I've solved it. And like all good stories, mine has a happy ending. It's about how this company will live happily ever after on the big profits they'll make with my swell new product.

At some point in your presentation, you have to be prepared to show why the prospect should manufacture and distribute your product. It's not enough just to say that the company will make money with it. That's the obvious reason for the meeting. You have to explain how and why there will be a profit. If you'll recall, earlier on in the CRASH process, at a certain point you had to evaluate your idea carefully before deciding whether or not to proceed with its development. The same factors that swayed you then can be used to sway your prospect now, except now you state them as conclusions rather than questions. Here are eight pretty good things to say about your new product idea:

1. There's a real need for this product.

2. The improvement over what exists is obvious, apparent, and beneficial.

3. The consumer will be sold on its advantages without special education.

4. The market potential is large and lucrative.

5. The market is easily identifiable.

6. The market can easily be reached.

7. The tooling costs are in line with the profit potential.

8. The spread between the true cost and the optimum selling price will allow for an acceptable profit.

Everybody Likes a Good Story

"Once Upon a Time I Had This Terrific Idea . . ."

Naturally, you'll add or subtract points to fit your particular product, but by the time you're finished, you'll hope to have Stu nodding his head in agreement so fast that he'll get a headache.

But wait, if you have the time, go to the business section of your nearby bookstore and look at all the books available on salesmanship. There are tons of them, and each is written by a supersalesperson who guarantees to turn you into one. Every book promises to reveal the one secret of sales success that has never before been uttered in public. The funny thing is that all these books tell you the same secret. For instance, you'll find the secret buried on page 127 of Herbert "Flash" Gordon's book, *Sales Stories from Hell.* It's on page 91 of Norman "Genghis" Khan's book, *Selling Door to Door in Beverly Hills.* And you'll find it revealed on page 142 of Wilbert "Whiz" Banger's book, *Famous District Sales Managers throughout the Ages.* Flash is a great salesperson and so is Genghis. And Whiz is probably more successful than Flash and Genghis put together, so I know that what they have to tell us is true:

> *The most important secret to sales stardom is to think from the customer's point of view and tailor your presentation accordingly.*

Who can argue with this? As one businessperson pointed out, "People don't want 1/4-inch drills, they want 1/4-inch holes." If you understand what benefits the prospect is *really* looking for in your product or service, and if you show how these will be achieved by buying your offering, then you, too, can write a book on salesmanship. Apparently there's always room for one more.

It's a given that Stu is looking for profits. Also, since his company is a half step behind Ajax Outdoor, Inc., it doesn't take a genius to assume that he'd like to catch up to them. With that in mind, and heeding the supersalespeople's advice, you can slightly rephrase the features of your new product. Here are eight very good things to say about your new product idea:

1. Yes, Stu, because there's a real need for this product, you'll be able to get quick, profitable, national distribution.

2. Yes, Stu, because the improvement over what exists is obvious, apparent and beneficial, the sell-through in the stores should be sensational.

3. Yes, Stu, because the consumer will be sold on the product's advantage without special education, you won't have to spend money needlessly on advertising.

4. Yes, Stu, because the market potential is large and lucrative, you're going to make a fortune and Sylvester over at Ajax is going to have a fit.

5. Yes, Stu, because the market is easily identifiable, your marketing people won't have to bother with expensive research projects.

6. Yes, Stu, because the market can easily be reached, you'll be turning over profits before Ajax knows what hit it.

7. Yes, Stu, because the tooling is in line with the profit potential, you'll have your investment back in months instead of years.

8. Yes, Stu, because the profit is there, you've got a megahit on your hands and Sylvester at Ajax will be so angry he won't be able to see straight.

This is called "benefit selling," and although I'm hardly in a superseller's league, I'm prepared to accept good advice when I get it.

The other thing any good salesperson will tell you is to *always* ask for the order. If the company representatives don't like your product idea, they won't be embarrassed to tell you clearly and promptly. If they do like it, however, you sometimes have to glean that from signals. Here are a few examples:

You Know It's Time to Close the Deal . . .

- When the conversation moves beyond the merits of the idea itself and onto more practical matters, such as production costs, packaging, and marketing.
- When the person you're meeting with calls another person into the meeting, and that person shows enthusiasm for the idea.
- When the prospective licensee has a pleased expression and keeps playing with your prototype with a proprietary air.
- When the other side nods and seems pleased with your answers to questions. This is particularly true if the questions have to do with projected sales volumes and profits.

Even when the signals are there for everyone to see, many people simply *hate* to ask for an order. It seems, somehow, to be the most vulgar thing you can do, even though it's understood that's why you're there in the first place. Stu may love your idea but is finding it hard to say yes. What with the economy being the way it is, and it's a bad time of year, and money is tight, and like, you know. What good old Stu needs is a gentle shove. This is when you say, "Stu, to be perfectly honest, I had already made appointments to show this to two other companies. If you tell me we have a deal, and if we can shake hands on it, I'll call them and cancel." Stu will never ask you which other two companies, and he hates the thought that a competitor would make a big thing out of something that he let slip by. It puts some tension in the air and adds a nice sense of urgency to the meeting.

Stu is just about ready to do the deal, but he wants just another moment. To give him a little more thinking time, you might have to go through this little drama:

Stu: So what about knockoffs? How do I know I won't be knocked off before I ship my first order *(assuming your product isn't patented)?*

You: Stu, if a pro like you ever worried about knockoffs, you'd never produce your first product. By the time the competition sees the item and tools up, you'll have a six months' head start. With your marketing know-how, by then you'll have our product in every decent store in the country, and they'll have to settle for the leftovers.

Stu: *(Stu already knows this, but doesn't mind a little stroking.)* Yeah, OK, so what's the deal on this?

The rest, as they say, is history.

A CUSTOMER'S TWO CENTS' WORTH

So far, everything we've discussed is from the point of view of the seller. I think it's worthwhile to let a buyer express an opinion. Tory Bers is a top product developer with one of the leading toy companies. Part of her job is to interview people with ideas to present, so I asked her for a few pointers. Here are some of the things she mentioned:

1.   *Make Sure Your Presentation Doesn't Look Shopworn.* If your presentation is wrinkled and dog-eared, it's obvious that it's been shopped around quite a bit. Nobody is going to say yes to a proposal that so many people have already rejected. The presentation must always look crisp and new, and every prospect must feel that he or she is the first person to see it. Surprisingly, I don't recall ever being asked by a prospect if this was the premier presentation. I imagine they assume it is because I always work with fresh looking material.

Most of the time, all it takes are new photocopies and report covers.

2. *Don't Oversell.* Make your presentation once. Do it thoroughly and with enthusiasm but don't get too aggressive. Be truthful and straightforward. You're dealing with experienced, professional businesspeople, so if you push too hard, you're going to make enemies instead of friends. When in doubt, pause to listen. Many times that will get you further along than talking.

3. *Be Flexible, Easygoing, and Helpful.* If you come across as rigid, unpleasant, and bullheaded, the prospect might fear that there will be problems in dealing with you down the road. If a customer is on the fence about your product, your attitude may be the deciding factor, so show your agreeable side at all times.

    The first lesson any salesperson learns is how important it is to be nice. When the caveman Zoggo, the world's first professional salesperson, first started in his career, he used to hit his prospects over the head with a rock to get their attention. Zoggo sold prelit bonfires, and sales in his territory were terrible. Finally one day, instead of beaning a prospect, he smiled and asked about the kids. The other caveman had never actually seen a smile before, but he knew he liked it and it generated warm feelings toward Zoggo. Sales for his prelit fires soared, and soon Zoggo was able to move his family into a charming three-chamber cave, where they all lived happily ever after.

    And since that time, over the years, the lore has been passed on from salesperson to salesperson: "You'll get more with a smile than with a whack on the head."

4. *Come to the Meeting Appropriately Dressed.* I read in the paper about a scientist who recently made a major discovery concerning the big bang theory of the creation of the universe. When he made the announcement to his colleagues, he did it while wearing a

tuxedo to underscore the importance of the event. A man after my own heart!

Businesspeople are like anyone else; they like to deal with people who look like them and seem to have their same values. If the meeting is in a big downtown office, and if you walk in wearing nice clothes and well-polished shoes, you flatter your host by indicating "This meeting is important to me." Underscoring the importance of the event, by inference, adds stature to the new product you're presenting. Someone who looks important surely must be selling an idea that's important.

Conversely, if you're meeting someone in a factory who comes to work in jeans, you'll make that person uncomfortable if you show up in a three-piece pinstripe suit. I had such a meeting last year, and deliberately wore a sportshirt and slacks. The individual I met with actually thanked me for not wearing a tie.

How you dress is a dramatic form of nonverbal communication. You tell people in an instant what you think of them and what you think of yourself. If they like what they see, it makes the rest of your job easier. If they don't, it's going to be uphill for you all the way. Although it may appear superficial, what you wear is noticed and it matters.

This is not the place to make a fashion statement. Earrings are out for men; low-cut blouses and tight skirts are out for women. Chewing gum is always a mistake, and I don't even want to discuss smoking. People look at you and form an immediate and enduring impression. I've read that in a social situation, these impressions are made in about four minutes . . . but in a business situation they can be made in as little time as *15 seconds!* But don't worry, with a little attention to your grooming, and a happy smile on your face, the first impression you make is bound to be a good one.

If you were applying for a job, and a secretary told the director of human resources that you were waiting in the lobby, the director might want to know what you look like. What the director really wants to know is whether you look as if you'll fit in. Like it or not, that's what it's about if you are a salesperson. Fitting in is half the battle.

5. *Cultivate Good Speech Habits.* I know I don't have to caution you about cursing. You needn't spend money on a book to tell you that. However, other patterns of speech that you may not have thought about are equally offensive to some ears.

All these personal points, how you look, how you dress, how you speak, may seem trivial in relation to selling a new product concept, but I can assure you they're not. At either end, none of this matters. If your new product idea is fantastic, its merit will come through even if you make your presentation while wearing a gorilla suit. If your idea is really bad, you can wear a tuxedo and talk like a member of the House of Lords, and still not make a sale. Most new product ideas, however, fall somewhere in between and require a degree of skill and effort to get them placed. And the first prerequisite of good selling technique is to create a favorable impression with your customer. The prospect who likes and respects you is more inclined to do business with you. That's where good grooming and acceptable speech come in to play.

For instance, excessive use of slang or teenage idioms sounds silly coming from an adult. It trivializes you and your product idea. Also, you run the risk that your customer isn't going to know what you're talking about. Always speak standard English and stay in step with your audience. If you are young and your customer is old enough to be your parent, you don't want to talk about the "modern" way of doing things and to thereby imply that your customer (the old dinosaur) may not understand. If your customer is thinking, "That little pipsqueak . . . " while you're making your presentation, then you've obviously lost the first round.

On the other hand, if your customer is much younger than you are, don't point up the age difference by constantly talking about how things used to be done before his time. Your customer will resent the inference and you will only have made things more difficult for yourself. The idea is to diffuse the age difference and, to the extent that you can, make this a meeting between two contemporaries who have come together to discuss an exciting new product idea. We don't talk politics, sex, religion, or race. We're here to take care of business. If you must make some small talk, discuss sports or the weather.

When you realize the value of first impressions and how quickly they're formed, you can turn it into a wonderful advantage. If you really concentrate on the first few minutes of your meeting, you can have the other side thinking you're bright, witty, charming, cultured, informed, intellectual, and all in all a very classy act. By the time they start to form a few second impressions, you might be out the door with a contract in your hand.

WHEN ALL IS SAID AND DONE

You have now completed your brilliant presentation and you handled all of these questions with flair and intelligence. You flattered everyone in sight, and they all loved your outfit. You made them laugh, and you made them cry. So now what happens? Now they tell you one of four things:

1. *"Thanks, but this product really isn't for us."* You naturally should accept this decision with good grace, but press for further clarification. Are they really saying it's not a good idea, period? If so, can they suggest ways to

make it better? If it's truly just not for them, can they suggest someone it is for? Can they give you a name? An introduction? There's benefit to be gained even from refusals, but you may have to dig for it. I long ago learned not to take these rejections to heart, and they don't upset me. It really may not be a good product (it won't be my first), and I either improve it or put it aside. Mickey Rooney said that you always pass failure on the road to success, and I know that's true for me and for just about everyone else who's out there trying. A professional attitude is to understand that there is nothing personal in these rejections. If you keep this in mind, and if you believe in your idea, none of it will get you down. Your idea truly may not be right for this prospect, but it may be perfect for the next one.

2. *"I like your idea, but I have to show it to my boss."* If it's at all possible, you want to avoid leaving your material in the hands of a screener. If a presentation is going to be made to the person who makes the decisions, you should be the one to do it. So say something like, "I'll tell you the truth, I'm so excited about this product idea that I'd like the fun of showing it to your boss myself. But I wouldn't want to do it unless you were there, so I hope you can set something up for the three of us. I realize how busy you are, so anytime that's best for you is OK with me."

   Although the person you're dealing with is looking to protect his turf, a flattering approach often works wonders. In fact, you could make a case for the statement that flattery works in almost any kind of situation. People never tire of hearing nice things about themselves no matter how outrageous they are. With a little practice, you'll soon be able to do it with a straight fact. So do whatever it takes, but don't let the assistant make the presentation for you. I don't recall ever being successful when I didn't make my own presentation to the decision maker.

3. *"Can you leave the stuff for awhile so we can study it?"* You have one of two situations developing here, and it's important to distinguish between them.

   A. If they want to keep your material for a week or so to discuss it among themselves, this is perfectly understandable. However, it's perfectly in order for you to establish a firm date by which time they agree to give you a response. It's important that date be clearly agreed to because you want to maintain a sense of urgency and you don't want them to dawdle. If they do, chances increase that they'll lose interest in the project. When they ask for time, you say, "I certainly can understand that you want to study it. I would too if I were you. There's a lot to think about. However, as you can imagine, I'm excited about the idea and am anxious to get it placed. So can you tell me when I can expect to have an answer?" Their request is in order, as is your response.

   B. If they want to keep your material for a month or more so they can build a sample and price it and test it and show it to their salespeople and to their key customers, that's another story. What they want is an option, and options are bought, not given. After all, you're giving up quite a bit by cooling your heels for a month or two while they put your product through its paces. You certainly are entitled to be paid for your troubles. The sum is negotiable, but the concept is that the money is never returnable. However, if they decide to proceed, it's reasonable that it apply against advances and/or future royalties.

   However the deal is arranged, it's not a good idea to leave your material on the spot. You should always tell them that you'll send it. There are three reasons:

A. You want to leave a paper trail so your covering letter confirms the meeting and lists the material being turned over for study.

B. The letter gives you the opportunity to once again stress the points made at the meeting and to reconfirm the date by which time they have promised to give you an answer. In the toy field, concepts that are accepted for study are usually held for about a month. If the company wants to hold it appreciably longer, it's acceptable to ask for a nonrefundable "holding fee" of a few thousand dollars. If the toy company decides to proceed with the product, the holding fee is usually applied against any advances that might be given.

C. Try earnestly to avoid turning over original material. Color artwork can be reproduced on a Canon color copier so it is almost as good as the original. It costs a few dollars per page, but it's worth it. Even the most well-meaning people may lose your work, misplace it, or throw it out. I've had expensive prototypes accidentally tossed in the trash on two separate occasions. Both times I billed the companies, and both times they paid with profuse apologies. But you never get back the article's actual cost, and look at all the time you lose.

   As I mentioned previously, I always submit my material by overnight messenger service or by the Post Office's overnight mail service. It's in keeping with the aura of urgency and importance that you want to maintain over the whole procedure.

4. *"OK, you've got a deal."* If you're dealing with a small company, you'll probably be working directly with the owner, who is an entrepreneur, accustomed to making quick decisions without committees. In that situation, it's not unusual for the owner to be ready to do a deal on the spot. So if you come prepared with a blank

contract in your briefcase, you may leave with a check in your pocket. If happens a lot.

In regard to making multiple submissions, there isn't a single correct answer. I can only tell you my system: I find the company that I think is the very best prospect for my new product idea, and I present it to that firm exclusively. Many times, it's the number two company in the business, on the theory that number one is fat and contented while number two may be a bit leaner and more receptive to new ideas. I tell them honestly that I've shown the product to no one else and that they're the people I want to do business with.

If they turn me down, I make multiple submissions to other companies with abandon. I sometimes have a proposal for the same product under consideration by three different companies. If company A buys it, I tell companies B and C that I am withdrawing the proposal. Interestingly, the next time I offer products to B and C, I usually get very quick responses.

After all the hard work you did to create and develop your product idea, it's a thrilling moment when a company executive offers a hand and says, "Let's do the deal." It may not happen on your very first call, but if your idea is sound, and if you persist, it's going to happen sooner or later. It's harvest time, and the right contract will earn you all the fruits you're entitled to.

6

Reaping the Harvest

Realizing the Most Profit from Your New Product Idea

*Whoever said money can't buy happiness
didn't know where to shop.*

—Anonymous

HIGH ROADS AND HIGHER ROADS

There are four basic ways for you to profit from your million-dollar idea. Some are riskier than others and some hold out a higher profit potential than others.

1. You can form a company to produce and market the product yourself.
2. You can sell your idea outright to another company.
3. You can license your idea to another company.
4. You can, perhaps, license the use of your idea to several companies.

Market It Yourself

Assuming you can raise the capital to launch a new business venture (which will undoubtedly mean pledging your home and other personal assets), statistics say that you are very likely to fail by your third year in operation. This is the killing time because most new companies are just one-trick ponies, and the third year is usually about as far as their original idea is able to take them. Typically, the first year is spent getting organized and launching the product. The second year is spent developing sales. By the third year, the original idea is stale or has been knocked off, and no terrific new ideas are forthcoming. The company spends all its assets scrambling to come up with something, and down it goes. I've been there and, believe me, it's a crisis event in a person's life that you definitely want to avoid if you can.

The Sad Saga of Little Teddy Ruxpin.　Some years ago, in 1984, a company named Worlds of Wonder (WOW) was formed on the basis of a terrific product idea that they licensed from an outside source. The idea was a talking plush teddy bear named Teddy Ruxpin. As he spoke, his mouth would move and his eyes would blink. For little kids, it was love at first sight, and Teddy took the country by storm. From coast to coast, guilt-ridden parents stood in long lines to buy this $100 toy because their poor children were the only ones in their neighborhoods who didn't have one. Scarcities quickly developed, crowds turned into angry mobs, and the company was frantically flying jumbo jets full of these little guys in from Hong Kong every day. Virtually overnight, sales rose to an unbelievable $1/2$ billion dollars.

Hot items in America have the life span of a gnat, and Teddy Ruxpin was no exception. His popularity dropped like a lead weight and Worlds of Wonder had nothing nearly as good to replace it. They scrambled to introduce one new item after another and had one flop after another. Meanwhile, the overhead continued relentlessly, day after day—salaries to pay, rents to pay, development costs to pay, commissions to pay, advertising to pay, travel expenses to pay. Within a few short years, the company was bankrupt and has since disappeared from sight.

We all know of new companies that have grown and prospered; it still happens in the United States and that's what makes our country great. Nevertheless, the overwhelming percentage of patented new products are never marketed, and most new products that are marketed fail, and most companies that are formed to sell them go bankrupt. It's commonly estimated that only one in a hundred start-up ventures has adequate financing. When I get a million-dollar idea, I'm happy to let an established, successful company market it. My house is safe, my assets are safe, and I'm not ducking any creditors. My share of the profits is smaller, but I prefer to take the money and run. Incidentally, that's what the people did who created and licensed the Teddy Ruxpin idea to Worlds of Wonder. They didn't start a company to market their idea. Instead, they earned more than $22 million in royalties in just over three years. That's not a misprint.

Sell Your Idea Outright

This is a judgment call, and you'll only know after the fact whether you were right or wrong. Obviously, this is the safest of all the choices and it depends largely on how entrepreneurial you are. It also depends on how urgently you need the money, how much confidence you have in the idea, and your level of faith in the company you've appointed to market it. Since we're already aware of the failure rate of new products, it's not necessarily foolhardy to accept a decent cash settlement and move on. But you never know.

The man who developed the concept for the G.I. Joe doll sold it outright to Hasbro, the big toy company, for $100,000. He recognized that boys liked to play with dolls just as girls did, so his idea was to develop a line geared to their tastes. At the time, almost 30 years ago, this was a revolutionary concept. His total investment was a few dollars to buy some samples to show Hasbro what he had in mind, the idea was considered quite risky, and $100,000 was serious money back then.

So it must have seemed like an incredible coup to be paid so much for so little. How was he to know that Hasbro would proceed to sell more than 200 million G.I. Joe dolls, plus many millions more in G.I. Joe ships and planes and tanks and guns and you name it? How could he possibly anticipate that he would have earned royalties on more than $1 billion in sales. And how could he have possibly guessed that, 30 years later, sales would still be going strong?

In another case, way back in 1898, a man named Joshua Lionel Cowen invented an electric flowerpot. It had a battery and a little bulb built in, and when you pressed a button, the flowers lit up. Not surprisingly, there wasn't a very big market for light-up flowers back then, so he sold the idea outright for a few dollars to his dear friend, Conrad Hubert. Hubert, being nobody's fool, immediately threw away the flowers and the pot they came in. He kept the battery and the little bulb and made a new contraption that he called an "electric hand torch." He started a new company to manufacture this product and named the company Ever-Ready. Do you think it's reasonable to assume that his friend Joshua might have regretted selling his idea outright for a few dollars? If he had licensed it instead, his heirs might still be collecting royalties.

To offset these stories, there are probably many more tales of companies that bought product ideas outright for large sums and were never able to make a go of it. Because the products failed, the stories are harder to track down, but you can be sure it happens every day. All you can do is weigh the facts available at the time, trust your instincts, and pray that you make the right decision. No one can expect you to do more than that.

License Your Idea to an Established Company

This is the most usual route and is the one I prefer to take. Over the years, I've had offers from companies to buy my ideas outright and I've always refused. Sometimes I was right, other times I was wrong, but in the long haul I'm positive I've earned more money by licensing than I ever would have by simply selling the ideas. My contract always includes an advance payment so I have some compensation if the idea fails (which is not uncommon). And if it's successful, I can hope to enjoy some of the fruits of my creativity. We'll look at contract arrangements in detail later in this chapter.

Multiple Licensing

Although very few ideas qualify for licensing in this manner, it's potentially the most lucrative method of all. You license your idea to one company and still have it to license to another, and another after that. For as long as it lasts, it's a perpetual motion money machine. Obviously, your idea would require strong legal protection, either patents, copyrights, or trademarks, and must have industrywide significance. If companies believed they couldn't compete successfully without access to your idea, they would line up to get a license. If you've developed something like this, congratulations. You've hit the jackpot!

Introducing One of My Foremost Failures. The most common area for multiple licensing is what is known as "character licensing." Snoopy from "Peanuts" fame is a character. Mickey Mouse is a character. A few years ago I developed a concept for character licensing that I named "Toga Tales." It consisted of cartoon depictions of Roman type busts on pedestals, complete with garlands and togas, except they were all hippos in assorted colors.

Each one had a make-believe Latin name and a recitation of his deeds. For instance, *Billus Maximus* was the first Roman attorney to win a IV-figure settlement in a chariot accident case, and *Flunkus Maximus* was the first Roman teacher to ever give a pop quiz. And I had *Auditus Maximus* for accountants, *Flossus Maximus* for dentists, and several other characters.

The idea was that these were to be awards for the "World's Best Teacher," the "World's Best Lawyer," and so on.

It was not the most brilliant licensing concept ever developed, perhaps because it was too complicated, but I did manage to sign up several manufacturers. The products they made with my license failed miserably in the retail stores, but because of the advances, I still managed to make a little money. That's the incredible power of character licensing. It's even possible to make some money if the idea is terrible. Character licensing has made fortunes for the owners of hot properties such as Peanuts, Batman, Teenage Mutant Ninja Turtles, and Trolls, to name but a few, so I was determined to try again.

Introducing Three Penguins from Antarctica.   I was mulling over some ideas without much enthusiasm, when I happened to see in the newspaper one of those periodic surveys that show American schoolchildren's poor understanding of geography. I have always loved the subject so it shocks me to read how little our children (and their parents) know about the world we live in.

That set me on a thinking course, and before long I had developed *The Penguini Brothers.* These are three little penguins named Amerigo, Vasco, and Marco. The iceberg they were playing on, at home in Antarctica, was swept far out to sea during a fierce, sudden storm. Alone in the middle of the South Atlantic, their iceberg melting rapidly, the boys were getting more and more frightened. They thought they were goners for sure. Suddenly, up popped Bertie, The Bottle-Nosed Whale, en route from Antarctica to Greenland for the winter season. Bertie offered to give the brothers a ride on his back and drop them off in Morocco (which was on his way). Bertie was sure that someone there would help the boys get back home. And so now the brothers are traveling from country to country, from continent to continent, hoping one day to find their way home to Antarctica. And wherever they go, they have a terrific adventure and also learn something about the country and the people who live there.

This is the way characters are born, with a premise to explain their existence and colorful graphics of the principal characters and the supporting players. I've now sold the concept to a publisher for a series of geographical adventure books called *Around the World with the Penguini Brothers*. The first offering will be a boxed set of three books with audiotapes and a special wall map of the world. If it's successful, more books will be produced, and the graphic imagery of the Penguini brothers will be licensed to various manufacturers of products for young children. And if it's not successful, I'll come up with something else. It's what I do.

I was willing to invest a great deal of time in the Penguini project because the profit potential for multiple licensing is quite high (but unfortunately the success rate is quite low). If your mind works in this direction, and if you think you can do it, I urge you to try. It requires a unique, creative story line, highly arresting graphics, and a great deal of luck. But if you succeed once, you'll never have to work again.

Every June an event called "The Licensing Show" is held at the New York Hilton Hotel. People with ideas like mine show their concepts to manufacturers who may want to put these designs on their products. Thousands of manufacturers attend, running the gamut from beach towel companies, to lunch box producers, to children's vitamin manufacturers, and each one is willing to pay great sums for a character license that captures their fancy.

As you might guess, this is not an easy field to break into, but the financial rewards can be enormous. If you'd like more information, resource names and addresses are included in the Appendix.

THE DOTTED LINE WALTZ

Since this book is about licensing, I'm going to assume that you will not opt to produce your product yourself and that you're not going to sell it outright. I'll also assume that, because your product idea is so clever and your presentation was so brilliant, the other side's ready to do a deal. You're not going to fall apart now. If you follow the next few steps, you'll breeze through the negotiations and leave the office with a smile on your face and a big check in your pocket.

The Gentle Art of Negotiating

A reporter for the *New York Times,* for a Sunday article, visited 12 stores on upper Broadway on the west side of Manhattan. None were chains and none were supermarkets. They were all individually owned. In 10 of these stores, she was able to negotiate a better price than that shown on the sales ticket.

> I love these shoes but they're more than I planned to spend. If you could give me 10 percent off, I'd take them right now.
>
> This dress is perfect, but it needs that scarf to go with it. I can't afford to pay for both—so if you could throw the scarf in for free—I'm ready to write a check.

I made up this dialogue, but I'm confident it resembles what transpired. It's negotiating. If you'll do this, I'll do that. It doesn't have to mean shouting, yelling, or grinding someone into the dust. In its best form, it's simply coming to a mutually beneficial meeting of the minds. OK, so you may hope, it will be a little more beneficial for you than for the other person. Nevertheless, it's a time-honored craft, and certain productive techniques have been developed over the years. Here are eight most important ones:

Know What You Want before You Start.   Before you even show up for your appointment, you should have a clear idea of what you want out of the deal. Each of your requests should be reasonable, well thought out, and defensible. By reading this chapter, you'll know each of the areas where the licensee may make demands and you'll know how to address them. Every time you hesitate or seem uncertain over one of the contract points, the other side will be tempted to take advantage. It's not difficult to prevent this from happening. If you know all the steps, the dance can be fun!

Don't Be Greedy.   I asked a half-dozen patent attorneys to name the biggest stumbling block in successful licensing negotiations and they all said it was unreasonable demands from the inventor. While there are certain bottom-line demands you must insist on, it's important that you listen and understand the other side's point of view. If you can appreciate the customer's true concerns, you can often accommodate them without sacrificing your own. In negotiating, as well as in selling, those who have mastered the art of listening have a real edge. It's pointless to continually make arbitrary demands that the other side can't concede. If you keep asking for the moon, you'll eventually get the gate.

An old Italian proverb says, "It's better to lose the saddle than the horse." The sample contract later in this chapter offers a clear, sensible balance between the two sides. It can guide you through the process to a satisfactory conclusion. And you'll still have the horse you rode in on.

Don't Get Personal.   You must develop a proper perspective about the negotiating process. Whatever transpires, it's not life or death. It's just business. Whatever the outcome, you'll still have your health, you won't go to jail, and no one is holding your firstborn for ransom. Therefore, it's never excusable to raise your voice or to be impolite. Amateurs may do that, but professionals never yell and never curse. They're never brusque and never rude. If you push, the other side will shove, and you'll soon have a brawl on your hands. What good can come from that? The purpose of negotiation is to resolve conflict, not to create it. People so obviously respond better to kindness that you have to wonder about the true motives of mean-spirited negotiators.

Postpone Conflict.   If you reach an impasse, don't go head to head to hammer it out. You don't want tempers to flair and to thereby create an ugly atmosphere for the rest of the session. Professionals put the problem clause aside as they work through the rest of the agreement. The idea is that when everything else is settled, and the end is in sight, both sides will be more flexible regarding the troublesome clause.

Don't Be a Patsy.   You must be prepared to make concessions, it's part of the process. However, you can turn this into an advantage if, on principle, you don't concede anything without a struggle. If you simply agree to whatever's asked of you, it unfortunately emboldens the other side to ask for more. You can halt this escalation by never making a concession without asking for one in return. "OK, if I agree to Point B, will you see it my way on Clause 6?" Fair's fair. "OK, I'll do this if you do that" is the essential spirit of negotiating. It's not about one side dictating surrender terms to the other.

The Fear Thing.   John F. Kennedy once said something about never fearing to negotiate, but never to negotiate out of fear. If you're prepared to walk if your minimum demands aren't met, and if the other side understands this, then you have a powerful bargaining chip. As you'll see from the following sample agreement, your minimum demands are so reasonable that you shouldn't want to do business with anyone who won't give them to you. It's a portent of bad things to come, and you'll be better off taking your idea elsewhere. You must never forget that people who can create commercially profitable new products are in demand. If this company wants your product, there are others who will as well. When you accept this as truth, it shows. You'll feel your power and so will the other side.

Win by Listening.   The other side is at the table because the customer's convinced that your idea will make money. Customers like this want to do business with you; they want to make the deal. However, just as you have certain core demands, so do they. There's no reason these demands have to be in conflict. If a customer says (or implies) "Take it or leave it," don't pay any attention and don't dig in your heels.

Your job is to listen carefully to get a clear understanding of what the other side really wants and why. Once you have this insight, it's often possible to restate the licensee's demands in a manner that you can accommodate. Or, you can offer "additional information" that will allow a face-saving shift in the customer's position. You're not out to beat them, you're out to accommodate them. The better you listen, the easier it is.

Don't Forget about Tomorrow.   Now that you're on the verge of licensing your new product idea to this company, there's a good chance that you'll be back with another new idea. If you create the impression that you're bullheaded or unreasonable, the company may think twice about wanting to go through this process with you again. Stick up for your demands, but always be pleasant.

Just as some of us, in our roles as salespeople, are embarrassed to ask for the order, many of us are also embarrassed or fearful to negotiate on our own. To some, it seems pushy and unseemly; to others, there's the fear of looking foolish or not doing it well. These are attitudes based on a misconception of what the negotiating process is all about. It needn't be a debate or a trial, and there aren't supposed to be winners and losers. If you understand clearly what reasonable demands you must obtain, and why you deserve them, you won't be a loser. And if you accede reasonable demands to the other side, your customer won't be a loser either.

Many people, including myself, enjoy the process very much. I never allow it to get personal and look at it as an opportunity for a frank, spirited, intellectual discussion. By the time you have finished this book, you'll also be able to do it well, and perhaps will also enjoy the process.

DO YOU USE AN ATTORNEY OR NOT?

The correct answer to this question is "I don't know." You have to do what your budget allows and what makes you comfortable. Naturally, if you are negotiating a major license involving great sums of money, it's prudent to have professional assistance. However, legal help costs thousands of dollars, and in most instances I honestly believe you won't get a contract as good as or better than the one presented here. My contract is a deal closer. When the prospective licensee indicates a desire to go forward, my contract will allow you to leave with a done deal, signed and delivered. Although I wrote this agreement myself (and I'm not a lawyer), it's been vetted by dozens of lawyers over the years and has never been successfully challenged.

Clearly, it would be bad advice to push you into negotiating without an attorney if you feel uncomfortable doing it on your own. After you've completed this chapter, however, you'll see that the contract requirements aren't all that complicated. If it's a simple deal, and if the other side doesn't have an attorney involved, you may feel confident that you can handle it on your own.

If negotiations reach a point where you and the licensee each have attorneys sitting by your sides, the nature of your relationship starts to head south. Your attorney begins with "What if . . . " and then proceeds to introduce a clause to prevent some dastardly deed that's liable to be perpetrated by the other side. His attorney counters with a recitation of the heinous act that you're sure to do as soon as the licensee's back is turned. And back and forth they go. You can't blame the attorneys, that's what you hired them to do. But the licensee sitting across from you, a guy that you used to like, starts to look like Attila the Hun. And in his eyes, you're beginning to bear an uncanny resemblance to Adolph Hitler. The chance that this will ever become a signed deal is now hovering around 50 percent, while the attorney's fee clocks are ticking merrily away.

WHO PROVIDES THE CONTRACT?

When our fictitious Mr. Stewart Bunyon of the Universal Camping Equipment Company says, "OK, so what's the deal on this?" it would be terrible if you replied, "I don't know. I'll have my attorney draw up a contract and we'll get back to you." The only thing I can think of that would be worse is if you said, "I don't know. Why don't you have *your* attorney draw up an agreement?" I shudder at the thought. Here are two reasons:

1. If you wait for the other side's attorney to take care of the agreement, the deal's liable to grow cold long before you get it. Terrible things happen fast and usually without warning. The person you're dealing with gets fired, a competitor introduces a similar product, the company's marketing plans change. You have to assume that whatever can go wrong, will go wrong. And it's all going to happen while you wait for the licensee's attorney to get around to drawing up an agreement.

2. If the other guy's attorney draws up the papers, I guarantee you it will be the Agreement from Hell. You'll be lucky if you don't have to give the licensee an advance as a gift, just for marketing your new product.

When Stu asks you what the deal is, you have to be prepared to tell him on the spot and, if he's ready, to do the deal on the spot. You should go to the meeting with a contract in your briefcase, just as salespeople carry order forms. And just as salespeople have to be prepared to tell customers the cost of whatever they are selling, you have to be prepared to tell your customer what kind of deal you're looking for.

If Stu asked me what I want, as I'm putting my agreement on his desk, I'd say: "It's a simple deal, Stu. I get $_____ advance against _____ percent royalty. The deal's in effect for as long as you sell the item. There's no minimum guarantee and you can cancel at any time." In just a few sentences and in less than 15 seconds, I've stated the heart of the agreement and told Stu exactly what he wants to know. How much up front? What's the royalty rate? What's the obligation? How long's the deal? How does he get out of it? That's it. Everything else is detail.

What follows is the agreement I use. I made it up myself. It wasn't prepared by an attorney. I have never lost a deal because of it, and I have never lost a

"Just a Simple Agreement"

court case in suing for my contractual rights. It's battle-tested and will enable you to do most straightforward deals on your own. If you should decide that you'd prefer using an attorney, understanding the contract will make you a better client.

Date: _____

LICENSING AGREEMENT

Harvey Reese Associates, located at _____
(hereinafter referred to as LICENSOR) has given _____
_____ located at _____
(hereinafter referred to as LICENSEE) the exclusive production and marketing rights to his new product concept as herein described and as per drawings, patent applications, and/or prototype samples previously submitted. In exchange, LICENSEE agrees to pay LICENSOR a royalty in the amount and under the terms outlined in this Agreement.

PRODUCT DESCRIPTION:

1. *ROYALTY PAYMENTS*

A _____% (_____ percent) royalty, based on net selling price, will be paid by LICENSEE to LICENSOR on all sales of subject product line and all subsequent variations thereof by LICENSEE, its subsidiaries, and/or associate companies. The term "net selling price" shall mean the price LICENSEE receives from its customers, less any discounts for volume, promotion, defects, or freight.

Royalty payments are to be made monthly, by the 30th day of the month following shipment to LICENSEE'S customers, and LICENSOR shall have the right to examine LICENSEE'S books and records as they pertain thereto. Further, LICENSEE agrees to reimburse LICENSOR for any legal costs he may incur in collecting overdue royalty payments.

2. *TERRITORY*

LICENSEE shall have the right to market this product(s) throughout the United States, its possessions, and territories, and Canada. It may do so through any legal distribution channels it desires and in any manner it sees fit without prior approval from LICENSOR. However, LICENSEE agrees that it will not knowingly sell to parties who intend to resell the product(s) outside of the licensed territory.

3. *ADVANCE PAYMENT*

Upon execution of this Agreement, LICENSEE will make a nonrefundable payment to LICENSOR of $_____, which shall be construed as an advance against future earned royalties.

4. *COPYRIGHT, PATENT, AND TRADEMARK NOTICES*

LICENSEE agrees that on the product, its packaging and collateral material there will be printed notices of any patents issued or pending and applicable trademark and/or copyright notices showing the LICENSOR as the owner of said patents, trademarks or copyrights under exclusive license to LICENSEE.

In the event there has been no previous registration or patent application for the licensed product(s), LICENSEE may, at LICENSEE'S expense, make such application or registration in the name of the LICENSOR. However, LICENSEE agrees that at termination or expiration of this Agreement, LICENSEE will be deemed to have assigned, transferred and conveyed to LICENSOR all trade rights, equities, good will, titles or other rights in and to licensed product which may have been attained by the LICENSEE. Any such transfer shall be without consideration other than as specified in this Agreement.

5. TERMS AND WARRANTS

This Agreement shall be considered to be in force for so long as LICENSEE continues to sell the original product line or subsequent extensions and/or variations thereof. However, it is herein acknowledged that LICENSEE has made no warrants to LICENSOR in regard to minimum sales and/or royalty payment guarantees. Further, LICENSOR agrees that, for the life of this Agreement, he will not create and/or provide directly competitive products to another manufacturer or distributor without giving the right of first refusal to LICENSEE.

6. PRODUCT DESIGNS

LICENSOR agrees to furnish conceptual product designs, if requested, for the initial product line and all subsequent variations and extensions at no charge to LICENSEE. In addition, if requested, LICENSOR will assist in the design of packaging, point-of-purchase material, displays, etc. at no charge to LICENSEE. However, costs for finished art, photography, typography, mechanical preparation, etc. will be borne by LICENSEE.

7. QUALITY OF MERCHANDISE

LICENSEE agrees that Licensed product(s) will be produced and distributed in accordance with federal, state and local laws. LICENSEE further agrees to submit a sample of said product(s), its cartons, containers, and packing material to LICENSOR for approval (which approval shall not be reasonably upheld). Any item not specifically disapproved at the end of fifteen (15) working days after submission shall be deemed to be approved. The product(s) may not thereafter be materially changed with approval of the LICENSOR.

8. *DEFAULT, BANKRUPTCY, VIOLATION, ETC.*

A. In the event LICENSEE does not commence to manufacture, distribute and sell licensed product(s) within _____ months after the execution of this Agreement, LICENSOR, in addition to all other remedies available to him, shall have the option of canceling this Agreement. Should this event occur, to be activated by registered letter, LICENSEE agrees not to continue with the product's development and is obligated to return all prototype samples and drawings to LICENSOR.

B. In the event LICENSEE files a petition in bankruptcy, or if the LICENSEE becomes insolvent, or makes an assignment for the benefit of creditors, the license granted hereunder shall terminate automatically without the requirement of a written notice. No further sales of licensed product(s) may be made by LICENSEE, its receivers, agents, administrators or assigns without the express written approval of the LICENSOR.

C. If LICENSEE shall violate any other obligations under the terms of this Agreement, and upon receiving written notice of such violation by LICENSOR, LICENSEE shall have thirty (30) days to remedy such violation. If this has not been done, LICENSOR shall have the option of canceling the Agreement upon ten (10) days written notice. If this event occurs, all sales activity must cease and any royalties owing are immediately due.

9. *LICENSEE'S RIGHT TO TERMINATE*

Notwithstanding anything contained in this Agreement, LICENSEE shall have the absolute right to cancel this Agreement at any time by notifying LICENSOR of his decision in writing to discontinue the sale of the product(s) covered by this Agreement. This cancellation shall be without recourse from LICENSOR other than for the collection of any royalty payment that may be due him.

10. *INDEMNIFICATION*

LICENSEE agrees to obtain, at its own expense, product liability insurance for at least $1,000,000 combined single unit for LICENSEE and LICENSOR against claims, suits, loss or damage arising out of any alleged defect in the licensed product(s). As proof of such insurance, LICENSEE will submit to LICENSOR a fully paid certificate of insurance naming LICENSOR as an insured party. This submission is to be made before any licensed product is distributed or sold.

11. *NO PARTNERSHIP, ETC.*

This Agreement shall be binding upon the successors and assigns of the parties hereto. Nothing contained in this Agreement shall be construed to place the parties in the relationship of legal representatives, partners, or joint venturers. Neither LICENSOR nor LICENSEE shall have the power to bind or obligate in any manner whatsoever, other than as per this Agreement.

12. *GOVERNING LAW*

This Agreement shall be construed in accordance with the laws of the state of _____ (Your home state). IN WITNESS WHEREOF, the parties hereto have signed this Agreement as of the day and year written below.

LICENSEE	LICENSOR
DATE: _____	DATE: _____

This is as brief as it's possible to make an agreement and still cover all the important points. Everything is spelled out in clear, layperson's language, and, point by point, the demands made of either side are reasoned and logical. It's a businessperson's agreement, designed to be understood and negotiated by you and the licensee in a friendly, professional manner. I once showed this to a patent attorney friend who told me that he could easily turn it into a tightly worded, 10-page document, but it wouldn't necessarily be any more effective than it is right now. Let's look at it more closely, section by section.

Introduction

In this section I identify myself and the licensee by name and address. I confirm my right and claim to the new product concept and I describe it for the record. I keep this description as brief and general as possible. It should be specific enough to absolutely identify the product but broad enough to encompass all the derivative products that may spring from the core idea.

Royalty Payments

This is the heart of the contract and there is no correct figure. It's usually in the 5 percent to 10 percent range with high volume items earning less royalty than slower moving products. Items such as toys, appliances, and textiles will usually be 5 percent or less. Products such as giftware and home furnishings are closer to 10 percent or more. If you can glean some understanding of the licensee's profit structure, it'll help you to arrive at a figure. Whatever you think is right, add a point or two to it. You may have a pleasant surprise.

Smaller licensees usually don't object to making monthly royalty payments, much like they pay salespeople's commissions. Larger companies, however, and those that license many products, are usually set up to make quarterly payments. This is not unreasonable, and I'm prepared to concede the point. Anything less frequent than quarterly payments, however, would be unreasonable. "Stu, the royalty is my paycheck. You don't get paid twice a year, so why should I?"

Some licensees will say that they won't pay royalties until they get paid by their customer. I explain that I'm not in the credit business and that's one of the reasons the licensee gets 95 percent of the proceeds and I only get 5 percent. In line with the principle of not making a concession without asking for one, I might suggest that I'll accept this payment method if he's willing to increase the royalty to 6 percent. That may only be one point, but it's a 20 percent increase.

It's important that the term "net selling price" be clearly understood and agreed to. You don't need hassles later on when the company sends you your first check. Simply stated, whatever the net amount of the money received by the licensee from purchasers of my product is what I expect to be paid on. The licensee can make any number of deals, but your royalty should be a percentage of the customers' invoices. Don't accept any other definition.

Some licensees ask to have salespeople's commissions also deducted, but I would never agree to that. If you let that go, what's to prevent the company from asking to deduct salespeople's travel expenses, or trade shows, or catalogs? Remember that your royalties should always be tied strictly to sales. Let the licensee worry about profits. That's why he gets the big bucks. Sales figures are absolute. Other figures, like profits and expenses, can be fairy tales.

My definition of net selling price says nothing about bad debts. Licensees almost never bring it up, but if they did, they would have a point. After all, if their customer goes bankrupt, shouldn't they be allowed to deduct any royalties you perhaps have already received? That sounds logical, but even if the customer goes bankrupt, the vendor often receives something in a settlement. And after your royalty has been deducted, the licensee will never pay you anything back from a settlement. Although I deliberately leave this out of the Agreement, I'm willing to concede the point if it comes up. Fortunately, it almost never does. Make the concession if you must. It's small potatoes.

This provision also allows me to be reimbursed for legal fees if I have to sue the licensee to get paid. Sometimes a licensee's attorney will stipulate that they're only obligated to pay if my suit is successful. I concede this point if it arises. I understand the intent is simply to head off frivolous suits. It's not a big deal so you can be generous. This is really a terrific clause for the licensor. I've successfully exercised it a few times over the years when licensees started to forget to send me my checks. The licensee can't object to the clause's inclusion because that would be an admission of intent to skip payments. In fact, I'd be wary about dealing with any potential licensee who did raise objections.

This clause was a later addition to the contract after I had a collection problem and found my legal fees were almost as large as the sum I finally collected. There are people out there who will simply refuse to pay because they think you won't go to the expense of bringing suit. However, when they're obligated to paying your legal bill, they usually have a miraculous change of attitude. Dorothy Parker once remarked that the two most beautiful words in the English language are "check enclosed." This clause can help a lot to make that happen.

Territory

Unless the licensee has a strong export program, I usually limit the license to the United States and Canada (now considered a contiguous market). If you have foreign patents on your product, and if it's already being successfully distributed in the United States, foreign companies will find you to request a license. If you don't want to wait for that, you can contact the trade departments at the embassies of the countries you're interested in. They'll be happy to provide you with the names of likely candidates and you can contact them directly. However, don't attempt a licensing deal with an offshore company without having legal representation in that country. This is one instance where you definitely can't do it yourself.

On the other hand, if your licensee is an international company, why not let them go all the way? What you can do is establish a separate export sales goal, and if the export department doesn't reach it, you can have the right to remove that portion of the territory. Licensees will agree because they won't want to be bothered with foreign sales either, unless the numbers are significant. If you do award foreign rights to the licensee, refer back to the Foreign Patents section. If you don't have foreign patents yourself, this is the time to request that the company file on your behalf.

Advance Payment

As with the royalty percentage, the amount of the advance payment is highly negotiable. Since there are no rules to follow, you can make up one of your own. "Stu," you ask innocently, "how many utensil sets do you think you can sell in a year?" Stu will probably give you an inflated figure, assuming it will make you more willing to make concessions. If he says, for instance, that he'll sell $1 million worth, and assuming the royalty has been set at 6 percent, you might say, "That means I can look forward to earning $60,000 the first year. Since advances are often set at 25 percent of anticipated income, suppose we follow the formula and set ours at $15,000. Is that OK?" I made up this 25 percent rule, but it's as good a way as any to arrive at a figure.

Stu may counter by proposing a $15,000 guarantee with half of it to be paid as the advance when the contract is executed. It's your decision. Either way you'll wind up with a minimum of $15,000 and, hopefully, much more if the product is successful. Whatever the figure, there must always be an advance and it must always be nonrefundable. If you don't have that, you don't have a deal.

Every once in a while, I encounter a company that simply *hates* to pay an advance and insists that it's "company policy" not to do it. I'm adamant on this issue and have always managed to prevail. I explain that this Agreement is nothing more than taking an option to produce a product. The licensee pays an advance to earn the right to tie up your product idea for months and months. If the company doesn't ultimately proceed with it, the advance is the penalty. The licensee wouldn't be able to get an option on a piece of property without money, so why should it be possible to do it with your new product concept?

Sometimes prospective licensees, desperate to avoid the advance, will *swear* that they are definitely going ahead with the project, so there's no need to pay an advance. If that happens, remember the words of H. L. Menken: "It's hard to believe that a man is telling the truth when you know you would lie if you were in his place." The bottom line is you shouldn't sign a licensing agreement without an advance. No matter what the company policy may be or what the licensee swears, if you can't get it, my advice is to pack your things and leave. Almost everything else is negotiable, except an advance.

Amazingly, in my own experience, at least 25 percent of the contracts I sign do not result in the product actually being produced and marketed. The developmental lead time is so long (anywhere from 6 months to a year or more) that anything can happen along the way. Perhaps the company's marketing goals change, or the company gets sold, or your idea becomes obsolete, or the concept proves to be too difficult and expensive to produce. Whatever the reason, six months later you wind up with the product back in your hands to sell to someone else. I've sold some new product ideas three times to different companies, and the products have still never been produced. At least the advance provided some consolation.

Copyright, Patent, and Trademark Notices

This is straightforward and will meet with no resistance. You're simply requiring licensees to put the appropriate legal notices on the product. This is for their protection as well as yours so they'll do it routinely.

If the idea you presented is in the Patent Pending stage (or not even applied for), you can negotiate to have the licensee pay the costs to acquire the patent in your name. The same thing applies to appropriate trademark and/or copyright protection. The argument is that the licensee's stake in the product is much bigger than yours, so its ultimately to the company's advantage to get all the protection possible. The firm may have house counsel, or attorneys on retainer, who can handle the legal work in a routine manner. My Agreement doesn't force the issue, but provides the option. The larger companies usually do it; the smaller companies usually don't.

Terms and Warrants

If your product is not protected by a patent or an unusually strong copyright, it becomes public domain as soon as it's distributed. At this point, it's usually not possible to take the product away from the original licensee to reassign it elsewhere. If another company wanted to, they could simply produce their own version (a knockoff) without seeking your permission or paying you a royalty. Therefore, in this case, licensing for a specific time period is moot. Because my products usually fit into this category, my Agreement makes no provision for time period exclusivity. But that doesn't mean that yours can't.

If the product you're licensing has sufficient legal protection, it certainly makes sense for you to place a time limit on the license. The licensee is entitled to an original license of at least development time plus 12 to 18 months. It's only fair to give the firm sufficient time to recoup the initial investment. Beyond that, if the company is not performing up to pre-established goals, you should have the right to look elsewhere. If goals are being met, the original Agreement should automatically renew for another 12 to 18 months, and new goals should be established for review at the next renewal period. Notwithstanding all of this, the licensee retains the right to cancel whenever it appears unprofitable to continue.

Assuming you have not established a time frame, my Agreement is designed to remain in effect indefinitely. If the licensee continues to produce your product for a hundred years, the royalty checks should still continue. Every month, when the mail carrier brings a royalty check, your rich great-grandchildren will talk about what a terrific genius you must have been.

The main reason this can happen is that the Agreement encompasses your original concept, plus all new products that may stem from it. If your original product idea has sufficient merit to remain viable over the years, it will undoubtedly be subject to continual change and improvement. Eventually, you may not be able to detect its resemblance to the original, but it's still your product and you're entitled to continue receiving royalties.

Product Designs

This clause is specific to my situation and therefore may not be applicable to yours. I have certain art, design, and marketing skills that I'm prepared to lend to the licensee to advance the salability of my product. The clause describes what I'll do free, and what I expect to get paid for. You may have other unique skills or knowledge that will be beneficial to the licensee and, ultimately, to yourself. For instance, it may be necessary for you to provide some technical training to the licensee's production people to aid in the engineering of your product. Will you do it free? Do you expect to be paid? This is the clause where you make these matters clear.

Quality of the Merchandise

The intent of this clause is obvious; you don't want to see any junk on the market with your name on it. It's harmful to your reputation and will probably lower your royalties. On the other hand, you have to understand that the finished product will *never* look as nice as you pictured it in your dreams. That's why the clause says that your approval cannot be reasonably denied. If the licensee is already in production, and you don't provide your approval because you feel the mauve should be a little deeper, the company will sue you back into the Stone Age. It's the same as ordering wine in a restaurant. You can't return it just because you may not like the taste. You can only return it if it's pure vinegar.

Default, Bankruptcy, Violation, and So On

Paragraph A in this clause is critical. Without it the contract may be worthless. "How long is it going to take you, Mr. Licensee, to have this product ready to ship to your customers? Six months you say? Fine. Let's increase that by 50 percent and say that if the product is not on the market in 9 months, I have the option to cancel the agreement and keep your advance."

Without a clause like this, your precious product idea can be locked away in the licensee's dungeon forever and there's nothing you can do about it. Ideas are perishable. If you don't bring them to market promptly, they have a tendency to rot. So be reasonable with the performance time, but make sure it's in the Agreement.

Licensee's Right to Terminate

A licensee who is losing money on your product has the right to say, "Enough's enough!" and throw in the towel with no other obligation than to pay you whatever royalties are due. This has happened to me more times than I like to remember, but there are never any hard feelings on the licensee's part or mine. We both understand that new product introduction is a gamble, and as astute as we like to think we are, we guess wrong quite often. Licensees must have the right to back out whenever they want, or they'll never sign the deal.

Indemnification

Picture this scenario. You've created this terrific new product idea and licensed it to a Fortune 500 company. Sales are fantastic and the money is rolling in. A Bentley in your garage is starting to look like a prudent investment. One day, a middle-aged housewife in Snowshoe, North Dakota, claims that the product burst into flames, burned her house down, and inflicted third-degree burns over 40 percent of her body. Three personal injury attorneys were killed in the stampede to her bedside. The surviving lawyer is suing everybody who has ever had anything to do with this product, including you. "But hey!" you cry, "I just dreamed up the product. I didn't manufacture it!" "Tough darts," replies the lawyer, "I'll see you in court."

You tear apart your desk, looking for the Agreement. "Where is it?" Your wife says the last time she saw the file it was in the basement, under the supply of cat litter. You race downstairs and throw cat litter bags in every direction. Your two cats make a blood oath to get revenge. Finally, the folder! As you frantically flip through the pages of your Agreement, your eyes finally rest on Clause 10: Indemnification. A wave of relief passes through your body as you see the certificate naming you on a $1 million insurance policy. It's only then, while wiping your sweaty hands off on your Ralph Lauren leisure suit, that you pause to reflect on what a true genius you are.

No Partnership

This simply makes clear that you have an arms-length agreement with the licensee that's limited strictly to the terms of the Agreement. If the management get arrested for smuggling illegal labor in from Guatemala, that has nothing to do with you.

Governing Law

If the licensee is from another state, it's beneficial for the Agreement to be governed by the laws in your own state.

Legal costs are less if you have to sue, and judges and juries tend to favor the local party.

THE SINS OF OMISSIONS

There's a method to providing the licensee with a deceptively simple agreement. Several important points have been deliberately omitted. Their inclusion is not to my benefit, and the omissions are almost never noticed. However, if the points do come up, I'm prepared to address them.

Infringement Protection

Suppose you have a pretty strong patent for your Whatzit, which you've licensed to Amalgamated Global Things, Ltd. Your product is on the market, just starting to sell well, when Amalgamated's archrival, Ajax Trans-World Bettergoods, Inc., knocks off your product and introduces their own Whatzit. Amalgamated is screaming bloody murder and wants you to sue Ajax for the gold in the president's teeth. What do you do? A lawsuit might cost you $50,000 in legal fees.

You never, ever should sign a contract that obligates you to sue. That way can lead to financial disaster. And yet if you don't sue, Amalgamated can say, "So why should we be paying you a royalty if you're not willing to protect us from skunks like Ajax?" On the other hand, why shouldn't Amalgamated sue? After all, they're getting 95 percent of the proceeds, and you're only getting 5 percent. And besides, you're only one person and they're a big company. And so, suppose you both decide to sue. How do you split the costs? And if you win, how do you split the proceeds? I have the perfect answer to all these problems. My solution is to duck the issue altogether and worry about it only if Ajax really does knock off Amalgamated.

I've seen clauses in contracts that do address the issue, but the statements are so wimpy that they might as well duck it too. The clause usually says that licensor will have the right to sue. If he doesn't, then licensee will have the right to sue. And licensor agrees to help licensee, and licensee agrees to help licensor. And they all live happily ever after. As a practical matter, if a knock off does occur, and if it's important enough, Amalgamated will sue Ajax on their own, without asking for your participation.

Licensor's Title

Some contracts have a clause like this:

> LICENSOR will indemnify and hold harmless from all damages, costs and expenses, including reasonable attorney's fees which may be paid or incurred by the LICENSEE by reason of any claim arising from any breach of LICENSOR'S representation or warranties under this Agreement and the LICENSOR, at his own expense, will defend and protect the LICENSEE'S approved use of the product.

Let's assume you honestly believe the idea for the whatzit came from your own creative brain. The licensee believes you and signs the Licensing Agreement. The firm tools up, and starts to manufacture and distribute the product. Sometime later, it receives a notice that it is being sued by Ajax who claims that its own whatzit patent is being violated. The suit asks $2 million in damages. Amalgamated turns to you for defense. Do you catch a plane to Singapore, or what?

Ajax may just be causing trouble, but who knows? In any event, the suit still must be answered. Amalgamated says, "You got us into this. Now we expect you to get us out." Unfortunately, they have a legitimate point. The best thing to do is take the coward's way out by omitting the point from the Agreement. Voltaire once claimed that he was ruined twice in his lifetime, once when he lost a lawsuit and once when he won one. So duck this question if you can, and bite the bullet if you can't. If you've done your homework, chances are extremely remote that you have innocently violated someone else's patent, particularly to the extent that they have been damaged.

Patent Improvements

As time goes on, you may find ways to improve the features of your product. Normally, you would routinely pass these on to the licensee, particularly since they may improve sales and thereby your royalty.

But suppose you hate the licensee and are counting the days until the license expires? Do you want the firm to have the improvements? Morally, I suppose the licensee is entitled to them. But I don't see anything in the Agreement about it; do you?

Disposal of Merchandise

Let's assume that, after three years, Amalgamated decides to cease selling the whatzits because sales have dropped off dramatically but the company still has $150,000 in inventory. You can't expect the licensee to just dump this merchandise in the river. If it is sold to a closeout business, below cost, should you still expect to receive royalties? And how much time does the licensee have to get rid of the merchandise? It can't drag on indefinitely because you may want to place the license elsewhere.

I leave this out of the Agreement also because there's no benefit for me to include it, and it's just one more possible point of contention. And almost nobody ever thinks of it. Nevertheless, if it does come up, here are some guidelines to get through it quickly.

It's not unreasonable to give the licensee 90 days to get rid of the stock. Less than 60 days doesn't seem fair, and 180 days or more is unreasonable. Nobody ever argues with 90 days.

If the licensee is getting rid of the inventory at or near the regular prices, you're obviously entitled to receive your regular royalty. On the other hand, if the licensee is selling off the merchandise below cost, I think it's unreasonable to ask him for a royalty on the losses. Between these two extremes, you and the licensee should be able to arrive at a formula to reflect a decrease in royalties proportionate to additional trade discounts. For instance, if the licensee gives an extra 15 percent discount, perhaps your royalty should drop by 1 percent. With an extra 30 percent discount, the royalty drops by 2 percent. And so forth.

Regardless of all the clauses and negotiations, and sallies back and forth, the best contract is the one that's reasonably equitable to both sides and is executed and put into a drawer and forgotten. If you know clearly what you want, the negotiation doesn't have to be unpleasant. In fact, I rather enjoy that part of the process. I hope this chapter makes you comfortable enough to enjoy it as well. To guide you on your way, the following section summarizes the more important negotiable and nonnegotiable demands.

AVOIDING THE AVOIDABLE

Aside from the boilerplate provisions, the Agreement has 20 essential elements. Half of these are nonnegotiable. They should be in your Agreement as stated, or you're giving too much away. The other half require some discussion and negotiation, and you should be clear on your position before proceeding. A firm, positive approach almost always heads off problems. Following are the ten nonnegotiable demands you must have in your agreement:

1. The royalty percentage should always be based on sales, never on profits.

2. The definition of "net selling price" should never include deductions for items such as commissions, catalogs, trade shows, travel expense, etc.

A Few Mild Requests

3. You must always have the right to examine the licensee's books and records as they pertain to the sales of your product (you have no right to know the licensee's profits).

4. The licensee must include the appropriate patent, trademark, and copyright notices on the product and the packaging.

5. You must continue to receive royalties for as long as the licensee continues to sell your original product idea, plus all variations.

6. You must have the right to approve product quality prior to distribution.

7. The Agreement must include a date, by which time licensee agrees to bring the product to market. You have the right to cancel if this clause is not fulfilled.

8. You must receive a nonrefundable advance against royalties at the time the license is executed.

9. Licensee must provide you with accident insurance coverage for at least $1 million.

10. You must not obligate yourself to bring legal action whenever licensee believes the patent is being violated.

Here are ten clauses you must be prepared to negotiate with the licensee:

1. What percentage royalty will you get?

2. What is the extent of the territory you will give to the licensee?

3. What is the royalty payment schedule?

4. Does the Agreement continue indefinitely? If not, what's the term? Is there a minimum guarantee on royalty payments? How much?

5. How big a nonrefundable advance do you get?

6. Do you supply your expertise free? If not, what's the charge?

7. How much time does the licensee have to bring the product to market?

8. Who pays the legal fees to complete patent work? Who pays patent maintenance?

9. If licensee is sued for patent infringement, do you reimburse legal fees?

10. After the Agreement is terminated, what's the arrangement under which the licensee can dispose of the remaining inventory?

This Agreement is carefully crafted in clear language with an eye to addressing the legitimate demands of both parties. It's been tested under fire many times, so you and the licensee should be able to read through it and come to an agreement with a minimum of stress and hassle. Its purpose is to provide you with all the rights you're entitled to (and perhaps a little bit more), while also addressing the legitimate concerns of the licensee.

And now that you have an executed Agreement and a check in your pocket, it's time to go home and start working on your next million-dollar idea.

7

THE UNLIMITED POTENTIAL OF LICENSING

You may be disappointed if you fail,
but you'll be doomed if you don't try.
—Beverly Sills

This is a tough time for American manufacturers. Foreign competition is fierce, the economy is on shaky ground, and in every area of commercial activity, too many companies are trying to get a piece of the pie. This may be bad news for them, but it presents a wonderful opportunity for us.

BUSINESS IS BOOMING

When companies think they're in trouble, what do they do to increase profits? It doesn't matter if it's a mom and pop operation or a Fortune 500 company, they all try to do the same thing: cut costs and increase sales. And what does every worthwhile new product do? It either works to increase efficiency (cut costs) or helps to increase sales. That's no coincidence. It's why licensing is such a booming business.

And that's why it gets bigger and bigger with each passing year. It's a vital part of the world economy. Without having access to licensed products and technologies, many companies would simply cease to exist. If you've developed a terrific new product concept that will cut costs or increase sales, any company executive will welcome you with open arms and a ready checkbook. Just call on the phone and you'll be invited to come right over.

Throughout the book, I've tried not to automatically refer to new product ideas as "inventions" (although they may very well be), and I've tried not to refer to us as "inventors" (although that description might be correct). The licensing business is so much more than just inventors selling inventions that I didn't want to confine your thinking to just that one activity. The following examples make this distinction clear.

Million-Dollar Babies

An artist named Xavier Roberts from Cleveland, Georgia, developed a concept for a doll and licensed it to one of the large toy companies. The idea was that each doll would be presented to the child as being "newborn," with its own name and birth certificate. The child (through her parent) doesn't simply buy a doll, she *adopts* one. It's a simple idea that any one of us could have had if we had focused our thoughts on that area. You would think that, at least, one of the doll companies would have thought of it. After all, it's their business, and some of them have been around for a century or more.

With all due respect to Xavier Roberts, it doesn't take a genius to think up ideas like this. It's probably not even an original idea, but Xavier deserves to get all the rewards because he's the one who did something about it. He developed the idea, designed the doll, gave it a name ("Cabbage Patch Kids") and went out and found the right company to license it to.

Xavier is not an inventor and Cabbage Patch Kids is not an invention, it's a merchandising scheme. Nevertheless, Cabbage Patch Kids have accounted for more than $2 billion in retail sales, turning an artist from a little Georgia town (who probably couldn't care less about being called an inventor) into an extremely wealthy man.

Cold, Cold Cash

Iowa winters, as you can imagine, are brutally cold; and if you're a farmer starting a tractor at 5:00 A.M., it must make you dream of gentle sands and swaying palms. One local farmer, at least, doesn't have to dream about it anymore. He probably has a mansion in Hawaii.

A few years ago, I had dinner with sales manager for a midwest manufacturing company who told me a charming little story. One day, out of the blue, a farmer appeared in the company's waiting room and asked to see the president. Since it was a small company, the farmer was quickly obliged, and he proceeded to show a product idea that would dramatically change his life and enormously improve the business fortunes of this little firm.

What he took out of a paper bag to show the company president was a store-bought mitten with a little hole cut out of the front. In the hole was shoved a plastic windshield scraper from an automotive store. And that's all there was to it. The farmer explained that it was the best way he found to keep his hand warm every morning when he had to scrape the ice off his farm equipment, and he thought other farmers would also find it useful. He reckoned that if the company produced it in an attractive way, farmers would pay good money for it. Obviously, the fleece-lined mittens with the built-in scraper that the company ultimately produced had an appeal that went far beyond Iowa farmers. I can't begin to guess how many millions have been sold, but the sales manager told me that they ship the product to every cold-weather country on the face of the earth. I live in a cold-weather part of the United States, and hardly a Christmas goes by when I don't get one or two as presents.

The fact that nobody can get a patent for a mitten with an ice scraper stuck in it didn't deter either the farmer or the manufacturer. They signed a licensing deal and both are quite happy they met. The farmer didn't have to read this book to understand that anything capable of producing profit is capable of being licensed.

Every time you hear a song on the radio, someone is collecting royalties. Every time you buy a book, someone is collecting royalties. Every T-shirt a kid buys with a rock star's picture on it, or every baseball card, earns a royalty for someone. If you can patent your idea, fine. If you can't, don't worry about it. If it's good, if it's a money-maker, and if you find the right buyer, it's not going to matter.

How High Is Up?

No one can begin to estimate how big the licensing business is. Certainly, it's in the billions of dollars, but how many billions is anyone's guess. The only fact everybody does agree on is that it's getting bigger all the time. The nice part is that much of this money is going to average citizens with no more talent, brains, or ingenuity than the rest of us. It's going to farmers, waiters, artists, and accountants—all ordinary people with ordinary jobs. Maybe in my next book I can talk about how you made it big with a simple idea that any of the rest of us could have thought of first.

Thousands of new products are introduced every year, while thousands of others are quietly discontinued. Some companies that guessed right have grown to be bigger than ever, and some companies that guessed wrong have slipped into oblivion. However, those of us who earn our living by creating new products are always on the job to serve the newest batch of entrepreneurs as well as the established larger clients. We've risked nothing, so we're still here, quietly collecting our royalties.

There's No Such Thing as Golden Oldies

In our trendy, fast-moving society, new products are being devoured at an ever-increasing pace. Most of the products on the retail shelves today didn't even exist five years ago. New technologies destroy and create whole product categories in a single gulp, while our changing lifestyle makes products obsolete in a heartbeat. Every old product must be replaced by a new one. Companies believe that if they don't grow, they die. So the frantic search for exciting new products is never ending and it creates the best of all seller's markets for people with appropriate products to license.

The Old Products Graveyard

Two of the busiest trade shows of the year are the semiannual National Closeout Shows in Chicago. This is where America's obsolete products come to die, and the entire retail world attends the wake. Walking the isles, snatching up bargains, you might find a department store buyer from Zaire walking past a discount store owner from the Philippines, who just bumped into a bargain barn operator from Kentucky. Once U.S. manufacturers have decided to discontinue a product line, it's urgent for them to dispose of the inventory as quickly as possible. They need whatever funds they can get out of the product, and they need the space in their warehouse for new merchandise. There's an entire industry of closeout specialists who bid against one another with cash offers for the inventories of distressed manufacturers. You might be astonished how big this business is. And it's all to make room for the new product you've just developed.

I've been involved in several businesses over the years and have been exposed to many more. In my experience, I've never seen anything to compare with licensing for profit opportunity and personal growth advantages.

WHY THERE'S NO BUSINESS LIKE THE LICENSING BUSINESS!

There Is No Competition

There's *always* room for a great new idea. No one will ever turn you away because they already have enough ideas, and no one will ever tell you that your competitor has a better price. There is no competitor and there's no such thing as a better price. You'll deal with top management, and every company you license to is a potential repeat customer. You'll always be invited back when you have your next big idea. Boom times or bust times, it makes no difference. The door is always open. Can you think of any other business like this?

Virtually No Investment Is Required

The literal truth is there is some investment. You may have to pay for a patent, a prototype, or a photograph. But this is pocket change compared with what you'd spend if you attempted to market the product yourself. For the person of average means, the financial outlay required could hardly be described as "risk capital." It's hard for me to think of another business that has such a huge profit potential in relation to the capital requirement.

No Experience Is Required

Over the years, I've created and licensed more products than I can count. I have lots and lots of experience. Nevertheless, the very first product you create could very well be superior to any that I've ever done. The edge I've gained from experience has nothing to do with the quality of the idea. Who could teach you that? My experience has taught me how to repeat the creative process, and I know tricks to getting my new products licensed. Now that you've read the book, you have all the knowledge you need. The only things you must bring to the party are intellectual curiosity and a will to succeed.

There Is Unlimited Potential

If you apply for a salesperson job and they tell you it has un- limited potential, what they mean is that, if you're good at it and work hard, you can make a good living. When I say, "unlimited potential," I'm talking about the sun and the moon and the stars and the planets. Here's what I mean:

Heroes on a Halfshell

In 1983, two Army veterans used their discharge money to start publishing an underground comic book. It was a crude one-color affair that they sold to those little comic book stores you see here and there. It started as a gag, a spoof. To poke fun at the standard comic book superheroes, these two fellows created four turtles named after Renaissance painters. They were dumped into the sewer, as small turtles often are, and years later they emerged as full blown, teenage crusaders, ready to do battle against the forces of vice and evil. They were named the "Teenage Mutant Ninja Turtles."

For a long, hard five years, the creators, Peter Laird and Kevin Eastman, continued in this fashion putting out their comic book. Toiling away in their small town of Northamp- ton, Massachusetts, and continually going out to comic book fairs across the country, they eventually managed to build up a small cult following for their "heroes on the halfshell."

At about that time, a bright, knowledgeable young man named Mark Freedman left his job with a large licensing company to go out on his own. He named his one-man com- pany "Surge Licensing," and set out to look for clients to represent. Somehow, he came upon an issue of the Turtles' comic book and immediately recognized the licensing potential in these four little guys. He drove up to North-hampton and the rest, as they say, is history. Even in his wildest dreams, however, Mark couldn't have imagined that this would turn out to be one of the greatest licensing bonanzas of the decade.

The three young men—Peter, Kevin, and Mark—joined together in a licensing alliance that has made licensing history. More than $1 billion in retail sales of products with the Teenage Mutant Ninja Turtle logo on them has been recorded, and that's not saying anything about the income from two feature-length movies, record contracts, book deals, foreign licensing, and other projects far too numerous to mention. And it's still going on!

I don't want to even try to guess how many millions of dollars each of these young men has earned in royalties, but the amount obviously gives new meaning to the words "unlimited potential."

It doesn't matter if you create a new style of windshield wipers to license to the auto industry, or just a poster about *General Hospital*. The right licensee will be delighted to give you thousands or millions for your idea. We see or hear about new success every day. In the current issue of one of my trade magazines, for instance, there's a little article about Sega Enterprises agreeing to pay Jan R. Coyle, an American inventor, $43 million for the right to use his technology in the company's video game machines. Ho hum, no big deal, just another inventor collecting millions.

In licensing, there's no such thing as reaching a saturation point. It's impossible. The supply of new products and new merchandising ideas can never satisfy the demand. It's a contradiction of terms. The better the new products, the bigger the demand for more. The more exciting the new products, the bigger the demand for more. And on it goes. If this book has awakened you to the possibilities of licensing and made you think about your own potential, I'll be very pleased. Nothing would make me happier than to be partially responsible for creating a new batch of millionaires. That would make this book the finest new product I ever created.

8

MAKING YOUR LICENSING DREAM A REALITY

With money in your pocket you are wise,
you are handsome, and you sing well too.
—Anonymous

I once heard Jimmy Carter explain why he decided to make a run for the presidency of the United States. His answer seemed almost too simple, but it held a powerful message. All he said was that, as governor of Georgia, he had met many world leaders, and it had dawned on him that he was at least as smart as any of them. Once he realized that, nothing could hold him back.

What holds the rest of us back is our tendency to underestimate our own ability while we're overestimating the ability of others. Once Carter accurately assessed his strengths, his ambition and drive were unstoppable. Surely we can do the same in our own way. The components for business success are reasonable intelligence, some talent, a plan of action, and the self-confidence to see it through. You certainly have the intelligence, and I can assure you that you have more than enough talent. The book provides the plan of action, so if you can just add a measure of self-confidence, you'll be on your way. Just remember what the little engine said while chugging up the mountain, "I think I can, I think I can . . ." And he could! You have to see yourself as a success before you can become a success. You can be sure that little engine would still be sitting at the bottom of the climb if all he could say was "I'm not so sure I can, I'm not so sure I can . . ."

We are all familiar with the expression that if it quacks like a duck and waddles like a duck, then it must be a duck. But this concept also works for swans. If people act as if they are successful, and carry themselves as if they are successful, then they will be perceived as successful. We've all met people who, by the sheer force of their attitude about themselves, can project an image of accomplishment. Their self-confidence comes through and makes them winners. And we all like to associate ourselves with winners.

MAKING IT HAPPEN

If you tell me you've developed a commercially profitable idea for a product, I won't be particularly impressed. Thousands do it all the time. If you tell me you've retained a topflight attorney who at this very moment is applying for an ironclad patent, I'll hardly be in awe. The Patent Office is clogged with applications (they've issued more than 5 million patents over the years). But if you tell me you have a beautiful prototype, a drop-dead presentation, and appointments to show your idea to three different companies, I'll know I'm talking to a winner! If you have the confidence in your idea and the confidence in yourself to put your drawings under your arm and knock on doors, I know you're going to make something good happen.

All the patent lawyers I've spoken to tell me the same thing. The typical inventor dreams up an idea, applies for a patent, sends out form letters to maybe a dozen companies, then sits back waiting for lightning to strike. It just about never does, and all the person ends up with is a good-looking patent certificate to hang on the wall and maybe show off to friends. More than 50 percent of patents are issued to small, independent inventors, and very few of them are ever commercialized. Inventors often don't seem to have the courage and self-confidence to go out and sell their ideas. They try to do it by mail because that's easy, safe, and nonthreatening. Or, worse yet, they give their money to an invention marketing company that promises to do the work for them. The bad news is that these approaches seldom work. But the good news is that terrific things happen to people who get out there and do it! It's not that terrible things happen to people who won't make the effort, it's that *nothing* happens. The months and years go by, and every day their dreams fade just a little bit more. And one day, it's just too late. The world truly has passed them by.

WE MAKE OUR OWN LUCK

And so the secret isn't talent and the secret isn't brains. The secret is *action*. When you can get into action mentally, physically, and emotionally, and when you focus all that enormous energy into the small hole of a clearly defined goal, you'll take off like a rocket and nothing in the world is going to stop you. Calvin Coolidge once noted that the world is full of smart, talented losers. We all know people like that who are just sitting around in their safe cocoons, complaining about the good luck that happens to other people. They may understand and pay lip service to the idea that people make their own luck, but today there's something they really want to see on television. "And, you know, tomorrow I promised to go fishing with the guys and next week starts the bowling league. But I know you're right, and in the Spring I'm really going to get myself in gear." They're planning for failure while the rest of us are planning for success.

It's not difficult to realize why people who may intellectually understand are still unable to shake themselves loose. It's fear of failure. "Flop sweat," they call it in the theater. Many capable, decent people are so frightened of failure that they won't even try for success. A person who polishes and nurtures a dream may fear that by trying to make something of it and failing, the dream will be destroyed. And without the dream, what does the person have? Never trying at all technically keeps the dream alive. The person's deadly lie is to promise to do something about it "tomorrow." There's an old Spanish proverb that says tomorrow will be the busiest day of the year.

FEAR OF FLYING

Fear of failure and lack of confidence are caused by ignorance, and the obvious cure is knowledge. People who are afraid of flying, for instance, are helped by being taught about the workings of airplanes and the principles of flight. The more they understand how an airplane flies, and the more they know about all the reassuring backup systems built into modern aircraft, the less frightened they become. And when they know enough, flying starts to become bearable for some and actually enjoyable for others.

My most sincere hope is that this book will work in the same way. By knowing everything there is to know about licensing—how to get an idea, how to protect it, how to get a lawyer, how to get a patent, how to get an appointment, how to make a presentation, how to conduct a meeting, and how to write a solid agreement—you will have the medicine you need to get rid of fear and take action. If everything is known, then there can be no fear of the unknown. You may even find that what you are doing is fun. And there aren't many better things in life than being paid to do work that's fun.

When I set out to write this book I had three objectives in mind. By providing you with some insight into licensing, I wanted to convince you that:

- You Should Do It.
- You Can Do It.
- You Will Do It.

You Really Should Do It!

Demonstrating that you should do it is easy. Success stories about average people getting big payoffs for licensing simple ideas are all around us. A waiter in Seattle developed and licensed a game called Pictionary. So far, more than 20 million sets have been sold, and it's still going strong. Think about it. If a waiter can become a millionaire from a simple, clever idea, shouldn't you be wildly intrigued by the possibilities? I can assure you from long experience, manufacturers are *eager* to give you money. Just demonstrate that they can turn a nice profit from your idea. Surely that's not too much to ask. Besides, what have you got to lose? A few dollars? A little time? That's an awfully small investment when you consider the potential rewards. The worst-case scenario is that nobody will buy your idea. It's not the end of the world. You'll have benefited from the experience, and your next idea will be better. The best-case scenario is so good that I'll leave it to your imagination. Either way you're a winner.

You Really Can Do It!

Demonstrating that you can do it is a little more difficult, but I think we've achieved that objective as well. I'm living proof that an average person can win at this game. You win by participating. Achieving your goal is the trophy. Just think how many times an idea of yours eventually appeared on the market by someone else's effort. Suppose it was you who did something about just one of them instead of its always being someone else? Probably you would only have had to do it once.

Yesterday, it possibly could have been said that you have more intelligence and creativity than you know what to do with. But today you do know what to do with it. In this book is the plan. You just have to put it to work.

You Really Will Do It! (Won't You?)

I'm not sure if you will do it. That's up to you. Have you ever bought a motivational book? They're usually written by psychologists and they often sell in the millions. This is not necessarily a testimony to their effectiveness. It's a testimony to the wide desire among so many people to "finally get started." These books are 300-page pep talks and on almost every page they say something like *"Do It!"* or *"Go for It!"* But do what? Go for what? They don't tell you that. That's your problem.

The problem is that it's not the motivation that's lacking. If the people were lacking motivation they wouldn't have bought the books in the first place. What's lacking is a direction, a plan of action. By providing licensing as a blueprint for success, I hope I've provided the flight path. This is certainly not the only way to riches. There are wonderful books about real estate investing, stocks and bonds, franchising, and almost every other commercial endeavor you might care to attempt. Licensing, however, is the only one I can think of that involves virtually no financial risk, and the rewards can be as great. If you don't at least *try*, you'll be denying yourself a unique opportunity. You can have almost anything you want if you work for it and stay focused on your goal.

Licensing is the single best way I know of to earn big-time wealth with small-time risk. People no brighter or more talented than you are earning millions of dollars from their ideas. There is no better time than right now to get started; manufacturers are desperate for new products and new ideas. Nearly every time I sign a contract, the licensee says, "I hope you make a million dollars from this deal." And it is an honest statement, because if I make a million dollars, the licensee makes 10 million. So nothing would give a manufacturer greater pleasure than to send you a fat check with lots of zeros every month. The licensee will put 10 times that amount into his own bank account. So buy yourself a notebook, go back to page one, and get your brain into gear. Somewhere out there companies are waiting to give you thousands and thousands of dollars. All you have to do is bring them products they can make money with. A fellow named Clinton Jones once said, "I never been in no situation where having money made it worse." Let those be your words to live by.

Speaking of words, the lyrics of an old song keep playing in my head, "You can do it if you wanna, but you better know how." This book has given you the know-how. The "wanna" is up to you.

APPENDIX

PUBLICATIONS FROM THE PATENT AND TRADEMARK OFFICE

Before you even think about hiring an attorney or conducting a patent search, order the following pamphlets. You will make your subsequent legal decisions from an informed foundation, and you'll probably find you can do many things yourself that you thought would require an attorney.

General Information Concerning Patents (S/N 003-004-00583-1)

This 44-page booklet provides a concise, clear overview of how the Patent Office works, along with understandable definitions of the different types of patents, trademarks, and copyrights. It's written in a user-friendly style that makes you feel the Patent Office is there to help you. Which it is.

Basic Facts about Trademarks (S/N 003-004-00605-6)

This is very similar to the booklet on patents, except that it also includes all the forms you need to file your trademark application.

Patent Attorneys and Agents Registered to Practice before the United States Patent Office (S/N 003-004-00573-4)

If you cannot find an attorney to your liking through friends' recommendations or through your telephone directory, this is the definitive source. It contains more than 13,000 names listed alphabetically and by state.

Patents and Inventions: An Information Aid for Inventors (S/N 003-004-00545-9)

If you're undecided whether to apply for a patent, as well as whether or not you can do it yourself, this booklet will help you reach a decision. It also includes a step-by-step description of the entire patent process. The booklet has only 23 pages, but the information is solid.

To order any of these booklets, contact:

> The Superintendent of Documents
> U.S. Government Printing Office
> Washington, DC 20402

It is also possible to order these materials through your closest U.S. Government Bookstore. If you have Visa or MasterCard, you can do it by telephone. Call 202-783-3238 between 8 A.M. and 4 P.M. Eastern Time. Or you can fax your order 24 hours a day, 7 days a week, to 202-512-2233. If one of the government bookstores is located near you, I think you'll enjoy browsing through their selections. The addresses and phone numbers of these stores are as follows:

U.S. GOVERNMENT BOOKSTORES

ATLANTA
Room 100, Federal Building
275 Peach Street, NE
P.O. Box 56445
Atlanta, GA 30343
404-331-6947

BIRMINGHAM
O'Neill Building
2021 Third Avenue North
Birmingham, AL 35203
205-731-1056

BOSTON
T.P. O'Neill Federal Building
10 Causeway Street, Room 179
Boston, MA 02222
617-720-4180

CHICAGO
One Congress Center
401 South State Street,
   Suite 124
Chicago, IL 60605
312-353-5133

CLEVELAND
Room 1653, Federal Building
1240 East Ninth Street
Cleveland, OH 44199
216-522-4922

COLUMBUS
Room 207, Federal Building
200 North High Street
Columbus, OH 43215
614-469-6956

DALLAS
Room 1C46 Federal Building
1100 Commerce Street
Dallas, TX 75242
214-767-0076

DENVER
Room 117, Federal Building
1961 Stout Street
Denver, CO 80294
303-844-3964

DETROIT
Suite 160, Federal Building
477 Michigan Avenue
Detroit, MI 48226
313-226-7816

HOUSTON
Texas Crude Building
801 Travis Street
Houston, TX 77002
713-228-1187

JACKSONVILLE
100 West Bay Street, Suite 100
Jacksonville, FL 32202
904-353-0569

KANSAS CITY
120 Bannister Mall
5600 East Bannister Road
Kansas City, MO 64137
816-765-2256

LOS ANGELES
Arco Plaza, C Level
505 South Flower Street
Los Angeles, CA 90071

MILWAUKEE
Room 190, Federal Building
517 East Wisconsin Avenue
Milwaukee, WI 53202
414-297-1304

NEW YORK
Room 110, Federal Building
26 Federal Plaza
New York, NY 10278
212-264-3825

PHILADELPHIA
Robert Morris Building
100 North Seventeenth Street
Philadelphia, PA 19103
215-597-0677

PITTSBURGH
Room 118, Federal Building
1000 Liberty Avenue
Pittsburgh, PA 15222
412-644-2721

PORTLAND
1305 SW First Avenue
Portland, OR 97201
503-221-6217

PUEBLO
World Savings Building
720 North Main Street
Pueblo, CO 81003
719-544-3142

SAN FRANCISCO
Room 1023, Federal Building
450 Golden Gate Avenue
San Francisco, CA 94102
415-252-5334

SEATTLE
Room 194, Federal Building
915 Second Avenue
Seattle, WA 98174
206-553-4271

WASHINGTON, DC, and
   Vicinity
Government Printing Office
710 North Capitol Street, NW
Washington, DC 20401
202-512-0132

Farragut West
1510 H Street, NW
Washington, DC 20005
202-653-5075

Retail Outlet
8660 Cherry Lane
Laurel, MD 20707
301-953-7974

INFORMATION FROM THE COPYRIGHT OFFICE

As with the PTO, the booklets from the Copyright Office are clearly written and contain valuable information. Also, they include the forms and line-by-line instructions for you to file for copyright protection quickly and easily. To proceed, you'll need *Copyright Basics* (Circular No. 1) and *Copyright Notice* (Circular No. 3). There is also available a range of booklets applicable to specific fields. For instance, there's a special booklet just for games.

To order, call the Forms and Publications Hotline, 202-707-9100, or write to:

> Copyright Office
> Publications Section, LM-455
> Library of Congress
> Washington, DC 20559

To speak with an information specialist or to request further information, call 202-707-3000, or write to the Information Section, LM 401, at the preceding address.

For your guidance, I quote the following from one of their booklets:

The Copyright Office is not permitted to give legal advice. If you need advice or guidance on matters such as disputes over the ownership of a copyright, suits against possible infringers, the procedure for getting work published, or the method of obtaining royalty payments, it may be necessary to consult an attorney.

Reprinted here are some of the basic copyright, trademark, and patent application forms which will provide a sense of the paperwork involved. As you'll note, they're all written in layperson's language and the information requested is quite straightforward:

Form VA is used for copyrighting published or unpublished works in the visual arts category. This includes drawings, paintings, photographs, prints, maps, charts, technical drawings, diagrams, models, and so on.

Form TX is used to copyright published or unpublished non-dramatic works. This includes fiction, nonfiction, poetry, textbooks, reference works, directories, advertising copy, computer programs, and so on.

PTO Form FB-A4 10 is used to inform the PTO that you are an independent inventor and, as such, are entitled to pay reduced fees for your patent application. The government believes that you should not be asked to pay the same rate as, say, General Motors.

If you are using an attorney to handle your patent application, *PTO Form 1579* is used to legally empower the attorney to act on your behalf.

The *Patent Application Transmittal Letter* accompanies your check for the patent application costs, along with the appropriate claims, drawings, and power of attorney.

The *Amendment Transmittal Letter* is used when changes or deletions are made in the claims stated for your invention in the original patent application.

PTO Form 1478 is used to register a commercial trademark or logo. These are words, symbols, or designs which identify the goods and services of one party from another.

SUPPLIER'S NONDISCLOSURE AGREEMENT

If you intend to use the services of a model maker, a photographer, an artist, or another professional and if it necessitates turning over secret or confidential information, you may want to have the person sign an agreement like this:

Date: _____

This agreement between _____ (hereinafter referred to as INVENTOR) and _____ (hereinafter referred to as SUPPLIER) is entered into under the following terms and conditions:

INVENTOR agrees to retain SUPPLIER to perform the work described here at the specified price herein quoted: _____

_____

_____

To enable SUPPLIER to perform these services, it is necessary for INVENTOR to provide certain secret or confidential information (herein referred to as the "Subject Matter") relating to his invention or product concept concerning _____.

1. SUPPLIER agrees to use this information strictly for the purpose of performing his service to the INVENTOR and agrees to hold it in the strictest confidence at all times.

2. SUPPLIER agrees to not reveal, publish or communicate the Subject Matter except to those employees required to provide the contracted service. At no time may the SUPPLIER disclose the Subject Matter to any other party for any purpose without the written consent of the INVENTOR.

3. All work done by the SUPPLIER in connection with the Subject Matter, whether or not registerable or patentable, is and shall remain the sole and exclusive property of the INVENTOR.

4. Upon completion of the assignment, SUPPLIER agrees to return all material and objects that may have been provided by the INVENTOR, plus any copies that he may have made.

5. If portions of the Subject Matter are already in the public domain, or if SUPPLIER can document that he has prior knowledge of the material from another source, he is not obligated to hold that specific material in confidence.

6. Except for possible exclusions indicated in Point 5, this Agreement shall be in force for five years commencing with the above date. After this time, the obligations of confidentiality are canceled.

This Agreement shall be constructed in accordance with the laws of the state of _____, and contains the entire understanding of the parties hereto.

IN WITNESS WHEREOF, the parties have indicated their agreement to all of the above terms by signing and dating where below indicated.

INVENTOR	SUPPLIER
DATE	DATE

INVENTORS' ORGANIZATIONS

The following names and addresses of more than 100 organizations are taken from available lists; their inclusion here does not represent an endorsement. Club members I've met over the years, however, have always been interesting, informed and helpful. Joining a local organization may be a productive way to secure information about patent attorneys, licensing agents, model makers, photographers, and other allied service providers. It may also be an excellent way to network your way into an appointment with someone you've been trying to see.

Meetings of local groups are usually quite informal and are often held in restaurants or private homes. If you call, you will undoubtedly be permitted to attend the next meeting as a guest before deciding to join. Typically, membership includes innovators and inventors, but you'll probably also find a sprinkling of patent attorneys, venture capitalists, and agents.

Most national organizations publish informative pamphlets, bulletins, or magazines and will be pleased to send you a few back issues of their publications if you ask. Nearly all these organizations are serious, nonprofit dispensers of aid to inventors. A few, however, are run by commercial invention marketing companies, so check thoroughly before deciding to join.

ALASKA
Alaska Inventorprizes
205 East Fourth Avenue
Anchorage, 99501
907-338-5484

Alaska Inventors Association
P.O. Box 241801
Anchorage, 99524

ARKANSAS
Arkansas Inventors
  Congress, Inc.
Route 3, Box 670
Dardanelle, 72334

COLORADO
Affiliated Inventors
  Foundation, Inc.
501 Iowa Street
Colorado Springs, 80908
303-623-8710

National Inventors
  Cooperative Association
P.O. Box 6585
Denver, 80206
303-756-0034

Rocky Mountain Inventors
  Congress
P.O. Box 4365
Boulder, 80204
303-231-7724

CONNECTICUT
Inventors Association of
  Connecticut
9 Sylvan Road South
Westport, 06880
203-226-9621

CALIFORNIA
Inventors Assistance League
345 West Cypress
Glendale, 91204
818-246-6540

California Inventors Council
P.O. Box 2036
Sunnyvale, 94087
415-652-3138

Inventors Association of
  America
P.O. Box 1531
Rancho Cucamonga, 91730
714-980-6446

Inventors of California
215 Rheem Boulevard
Moraga, 94556
415-376-7541

Inventors Workshop
  International
P.O. Box 251
Tarzana, 91356

Inventors Workshop
3537 Old Conejo Road,
  Suite 120
Newbury Park, 91320
805-499-1626

National Inventors Foundation
345 West Cypress Street
Glendale, 91204
818-246-6540

Silicon Valley Entrepreneurs
  Club
Techmart Building, Suite 360
5201 Great America Parkway
Santa Clara, 95054
408-562-6040

Spirit of the Future Creative
  Institute
3308½ Mission Street,
  Suite 300
San Francisco, 94110

Women Entrepreneurs
1275 Market Street,
  Suite 1300
San Francisco, 94103

DISTRICT OF COLUMBIA
Intellectual Property
  Owners, Inc.
1255 Twenty-Third Street,
  NW, Suite 850
Washington, 20037

National Association of Plant
  Patent Owners
1250 I Street, NW, Suite 500
Washington, 20005
202-789-2900

FLORIDA
Central Florida Inventors Club
P.O. Box 13416
Orlando, 32808
305-859-4855

Central Florida Inventors
  Council
4855 Big Oaks Lane
Orlando, 32806
305-859-4855

The Inventors Club
Route 11, Box 379
Pensacola, 32514
904-433-5619

Palm Beach Society of
  American Inventors
P.O. Box 26
Palm Beach, 33480
304-655-0536

Society for Inventors and
  Entrepreneurs
306 Georgetown Drive
Casselberry, 32707
305-859-4855

Tampa Bay Inventors' Council
P.O. Box 2254
Largo, 34294

GEORGIA
Inventor Associates of Georgia
637 Linwood Avenue, NW
Atlanta, 30306
404-656-5361

GEORGIA *(Continued)*
Inventors Association of
  Georgia
241 Freyer Drive, NE
Marietta, 30060
404-427-8024

Inventors Club of America
P.O. Box 450261
Atlanta, 30345
404-938-5089

HAWAII
Inventors Council of Hawaii
P.O. Box 27844
Honolulu, 96827

ILLINOIS
Chicago High Tech Association
53 West Jackson Boulevard,
  Suite 1634
Chicago, 60604
312-939-5355

Inventors Council
53 West Jackson Street,
  Suite 1041
Chicago, 60604
312-939-3329

INDIANA
Indiana Inventors Association
P.O. Box 2388
Indianapolis, 46206

International Association of
  Professional Inventors
Route 10, 4412 Greenhill Way
Anderson, 46011
317-644-2104

Inventors Association of
  Indiana
612 Ironwood Drive
Plainfield, 46168
317-645-5597

The Inventors & Entrepreneurs
  Society of Indiana
Box 2224
Hammond, 46325
219-989-2354

KANSAS
Kansas Association of Inventors
2015 Lakin
Great Bend, 67530
316-792-1375

Young Entrepreneurs
  Organization
Campus Box 147
Wichita State University
Wichita, 67208
316-689-3000

MASSACHUSETTS
Innovation Development
  Institute
45 Beach Fluff Avenue,
  Suite 300
Swampscott, 01907

Innovation Invention Network
132 Breakneck Road
Southbridge, 01550

Inventors Association of New
  England
P.O. Box 335
Lexington, 02173
617-862-5008

National Council for Industrial
  Innovation
105 Charles Street, Suite 530
Boston, 02114
617-367-0072

Worchester Area Inventors
Club
132 Sterling Street
West Boylson, 01583
617-835-6435

MICHIGAN
American Association of
Inventors
6562 East Curtis Road
Bridgeport, 48722
517-799-8208

Inventors Association of Metro
Detroit
19813 East Nine Mile Road
St. Clair Shores, 48080
303-772-7888

Inventors Council of Michigan
Institute of Science and
Technology
220 Bonisteel Boulevard
Ann Arbor, 48109

MINNESOTA
Inno-Media
230 Tenth Avenue, South
Minneapolis, 55415
612-342-4311

Inventors Club of Minnesota
P.O. Box 14-235
St. Paul, 55114
612-379-7387

Inventors Education Network
P.O. Box 14775
Minneapolis, 55414
612-379-7387

Minneapolis Entrepreneurs
Club
511 Eleventh Avenue, South
Minneapolis, 55415

Minnesota Inventors Congress
P.O. Box 71
Redwood Falls, 56283

Minnesota Project
Innovation, Inc.
Hazeltine Gates Office Building
Chaska, 55318
612-448-8826

Rolling Inventors Education
Network
P.O. Box 14775
Minneapolis, 55414

Society of Minnesota Inventors
20231 Basalt Street, NW
Anoka, 55303

MISSISSIPPI
Confederacy of Mississippi
Inventors
4759 Nailor Road
Vicksburg, 39180
601-636-6561

Inventors Workshop
1021 Cedar Hill Drive
Jackson, 39206
601-362-2968

Inventors Workshop
P.O. Box 4398
Meridian, 39304
601-483-8241

Inventors Workshop
P.O. Box 1268
Gulfport, 39502
601-865-0010

Mississippi Inventors
Workshop
4729 Kings Highway
Jackson, 39206
601-366-3661

MISSISSIPPI *(Continued)*
Mississippi Research and
    Development Center
3825 Ridgewood Road
Jackson, 39211
601-366-3661

Society of Mississippi
    Inventors
P.O. Box 5111
Jackson, 39296
601-984-6047

MISSOURI
Inventors Association of
    St. Louis
P.O. Box 16544
St. Louis, 63105
314-534-2677

Missouri Inventors Association
204 East High Street
Jefferson City, 65101
314-636-2026

NEBRASKA
Kearney Inventors Association
2001 Avenue A, Box 607
Kearney, 68847
308-237-3101

Lincoln Inventors Association
P.O. Box 94666
Lincoln, 68509
402-471-3782

Omaha Inventors Club
11145 Mill Valley Road
Omaha, 68145
402-221-3604

NEVADA
Inventors Workshop
Box 5531
Incline Village, 89450
702-831-2367

Nevada Inventors Association
4001 South Virginia Street
Reno, 89502
702-322-9636

NEW JERSEY
National Society of Inventors
539 Laurel Place
South Orange, 07079
201-596-3322

Society for the Encouragement
    of Research and Invention
P.O. Box 412
100 Summit Avenue
Summit, 07901
201-273-1088

NEW MEXICO
Albuquerque Invention Club
Box 30062
Albuquerque, 87190
505-266-3541

NEW YORK
American Copyright Society
345 West Fifty-Eighth Street
New York, 10019
212-582-5705

International Licensing
    Industry and Merchandisers
    Association
350 Fifth Avenue, Suite 6210
New York, 10018
212-244-1944

Inventrepreneurs Forum
Five Riverside Drive
New York, 10023
212-874-1626

N.Y. Society of Professional
Inventors
State University of New York
at Farmingdale
Lupton Hall
Farmingdale, 11735
614-797-4434

Inventors Workshop
126 Grandview Terrace
Batavia, 14020
914-248-5362

Inventors Workshop
RFD 2, Box 127
Granite Springs, 10527
914-656-9210

Inventors Workshop
205 South Central Avenue
Mineola, 13116
316-656-9210

NORTH DAKOTA
Innovation Institute
Box 429
Larimore, 58215
617-343-2237

OKLAHOMA
Invention Development Society
8320 SW Eighth Street
Oklahoma City, 73128

Oklahoma Inventors Congress
P.O. Box 54625
Oklahoma City, 73152
405-848-1991

OHIO
Akron/Youngstown
Inventors Org.
1225 West Market Street
Akron, 44313
216-864-5550

Columbus Inventors
Association
2480 East Avenue
Columbus, 43202
614-267-9033

Inventors Club of Greater
Cincinnati
18 Gambier Circle
Cincinnati, 45218
513-825-1222

Inventors Network of Columbus
Business Technology Center
1445 Summit Street
Columbus, 43201
614-291-7900

Inventors Connection of
Greater Cleveland
P.O. Box 46254
Bedford, 44146
216-226-9681

Inventors Council of Dayton
P.O. Box 77
Dayton, 45402
513-439-4497

Inventors Council of Greater
Lorain County
1005 North Abbe Road
Elyria, 44035
216-365-7771

Ohio Inventors Association
10595 Sand Ridge Road
Millfield, 45761
614-797-4434

OREGON
Inventors Workshop
20133 NW Morgan Road
Portland, 97231
503-621-3585

OREGON *(Continued)*
Inventors Workshop
780 SW 231st Avenue
Hillsboro, 97123
503-642-4122

Inventors Workshop
2876 Cloverdale Road
Turner, 97392
503-743-2002

PENNSYLVANIA
American Inventors Council
P.O. Box 58426
Philadelphia, 19102
215-546-6601

Inventors League
403 Longfield Road
Philadelphia, 19118

SOUTH DAKOTA
South Dakota Inventors
    Congress
Watertown Area Chamber of
    Commerce
P.O. Box 1113
Watertown, 57201
605-886-5814

TENNESSEE
Tennessee Inventors
    Association
P.O. Box 11225
Knoxville, 37939

Venture Exchange Forum
P.O. Box 23184
Knoxville, 37933
615-694-6772

TEXAS
Houston Inventors Association
600 West Gray
Houston, 77019

Inventors & Entrepreneurs
    Association of Austin
6714 Spicewood Springs Road
Austin, 78759
512-452-9043

Network of American
    Inventors and Entrepreneurs
402 Pierce, Suite 300
Houston, 77002
713-650-0645

Texas Innovation Information
    Network
INFOMART
1950 Stemmons Freeway
P.O. Box 471
Dallas, 75207
214-746-5140

Texas Inventors Association
4000 Rock Creek Drive 100
Dallas, 75204
214-528-8050

Toy & Game Inventors of
    America
5813 McCart Avenue
Fort Worth, 76133
817-292-9021

UTAH
Intermountain Society of
    Inventors
1395 East Greenfield Avenue
Salt Lake City, 84121
801-278-5679

Intermountain Society of
    Inventors and Designers
5770 Minder Drive
Salt Lake City, 84121

VIRGINIA
Association for Science,
Technology and Innovation
P.O. Box 1241
Arlington, VA 22210

National Patent Council
Crystal Plaze One
2001 Jefferson Davis Highway,
Suite 301
Arlington, 22202
703-521-1669

WASHINGTON
Inventors Association of
Washington
P.O. Box 1725
Bellevue, 98009
206-455-5520

Inventors Workshop
2702 Fortieth Street East
Tacoma, 98404
206-922-9032

WISCONSIN
Midwest Inventors Group
P.O. Box 518
Chippewa Falls, 54729
715-723-5061

CANADA
Inventors Association of
Canada
P.O. Box 281
Swift Current, SK, S9H 3V6
306-773-7762

Women Inventors Project, Inc.
22 King Street South, Suite 500
Waterloo, ON, N2J 1N8

PATENT AND TRADEMARK DEPOSITORY LIBRARIES

If you decide to conduct your own patent or trademark search, here are the locations of the libraries. You'll find the personnel are well trained, cheerful, and happy to help you in every way.

ALABAMA
Auburn University Libraries
205-844-1747

Birmingham Public Library
205-226-3680

ALASKA
Anchorage: Z.J. Loussac Public
Library
907-261-2917

ARIZONA
Tempe: Noble Library
Arizona State University
602-965-7607

ARKANSAS
Little Rock: Arkansas State
Library
501-682-2053

CALIFORNIA
Los Angeles Public Library
213-612-3273

Sacramento: California State
Library
916-654-0069

San Diego Public Library
619-236-5813

Sunnyvale Patent Clearinghouse
408-730-7290

COLORADO
Denver Public Library
303-640-8847

CONNECTICUT
New Haven: Science Park
Library
203-786-5447

DELAWARE
Newark: University of
Delaware Library
302-451-2965

DISTRICT OF COLUMBIA
Howard University Libraries
202-806-7252

FLORIDA
Fort Lauderdale: Broward
County Main Library
305-357-7444

Miami-Dade Public Library
305-375-2665

Orlando: University of Central
Florida
407-823-2562

Tampa Campus Library,
University of Southern
Florida
813-974-2726

GEORGIA
Atlanta: Price Gilbert
Memorial Library, Georgia
Institute of Technology
404-894-4508

HAWAII
Honolulu: Hawaii State Public
Library
808-586-3477

IDAHO
Moscow: University of Idaho
Library
208-885-6235

ILLINOIS
Chicago Public Library
312-269-2865

Springfield: Illinois State
Library
217-782-5659

INDIANA
Indianapolis-Marion County
Library
317-269-1741

West Lafayette: Purdue
University Library
317-494-2873

IOWA
Des Moines: State Library of
Iowa
515-281-4118

KANSAS
Wichita: Ablah Library,
Wichita State University
316-689-3155

KENTUCKY
Louisville Free Public Library
502-561-8617

LOUISIANA
Baton Rouge: Troy H.
Middleton Library, Louisiana
State University
504-388-2570

MARYLAND
College Park: Engineering and
Physical Sciences Library,
University of Maryland
301-405-9157

MASSACHUSETTS
Amherst: Physical Sciences
Library, University of
Massachusetts
413-545-1370

Boston Public Library
617-536-5400 (Ext. 265)

MICHIGAN
Ann Arbor: Engineering
Transportation Library,
University of Michigan
313-764-7494

Big Rapids: Abigail S. Timme
Library, Ferris State
University
(No phone yet)

Detroit Public Library
313-833-1450

MINNESOTA
Minneapolis Public Library
612-372-6570

MISSOURI
Kansas City: Linda Hall Library
816-363-4600

St. Louis Public Library
314-241-2288 (Ext. 390)

MONTANA
Butte: Montana College of
Mineral Science and
Technology Library
460-496-4281

NEBRASKA
Lincoln: Engineering Library,
University of Nebraska at
Lincoln
402-472-3411

NEVADA
University of Nevada-Reno
Library
702-784-6579

NEW HAMPSHIRE
Durham: University of New
Hampshire Library
603-862-1777

NEW JERSEY
Newark Public Library
201-733-7782

Piscataway: Library of Science
and Medicine, Rutgers
University
201-932-2895

NEW MEXICO
Albuquerque: University of
New Mexico General Library
505-277-4412

NEW YORK
Albany: New York State Library
518-473-4636

Buffalo and Erie County
Public Library
716-858-7101

New York Public Library (The
Research Libraries)
212-714-8529

NORTH CAROLINA
Raleigh: D.H. Hill Library,
North Carolina State
University
919-737-3280

NORTH DAKOTA
Grand Forks: Chester Fritz
Library, University of North
Dakota
701-777-4888

OHIO
Public Library of Cincinnati
and Hamilton County
513-369-6936

Cleveland Public Library
216-623-2870

Columbus: Ohio State
University Library
614-292-6175

Toledo/Lucas County Public
Library
419-259-5212

OKLAHOMA
Stillwater: Oklahoma State
University Library
405-744-7086

OREGON
Salem: Oregon Public Library
503-378-4239

PENNSYLVANIA
The Free Library of
Philadelphia
215-686-5331

Carnegie Library of Pittsburgh
412-622-3138

University Park: Pattee Library,
Pennsylvania State
University
814-865-4861

RHODE ISLAND
Providence Public Library
401-455-8027

SOUTH CAROLINA
Charleston: Medical University
of South Carolina Library
803-792-2372

TENNESSEE
Memphis and Shelby County
Library
901-725-8876

Nashville: Stevenson Science
Library, Vanderbilt
University
615-322-2775

TEXAS
Austin: McKinney Engineering
  Library
University of Texas
512-495-4500

College Station: Sterling C.
  Evans Library, Texas A&M
  University
409-845-2551

Dallas Public Library
214-670-1468

SMALL BUSINESS ADMINISTRATION

The principal mission of this agency is to provide information for startup ventures and for small business owners in areas such as financial management, marketing, and accounting. However, it does have publications that discuss Inventions (Order No. PI 1) and Patents (Order No. PI 2). They only cost 50 cents each and are worth ordering. Also, if you can find the time to visit your local SBA office, you may find other publications and services that will be useful. Here's where they're located:

ALABAMA
2121 Eighth Avenue North,
  Suite 200
Birmingham, 35203
205-731-1338

ALASKA
701 C Street, Room 1068
Anchorage, 99513
907-271-4022

ARIZONA
2005 North Central Avenue,
  Fifth Floor
Phoenix, 85004
602-261-3732

300 West Congress Street,
  Room 3V
Tucson, 85701
602-629-6715

ARKANSAS
320 West Capital Avenue,
  Suite 601
Little Rock, 72201
501-378-5871

CALIFORNIA
2202 Monterey Street, Suite 108
Fresno, 93721
209-487-5189

CALIFORNIA *(Continued)*
350 South Figueroa Street,
  Sixth Floor
Los Angeles, 90071
213-894-2956

660 J Street, Suite 215
Sacramento, 95814
916-551-1445

880 Front Street
San Diego, 92188
619-557-7269

211 Main Street, Fourth Floor
San Francisco, 94105
415-974-0642

COLORADO
721 Nineteenth Street,
  Room 407
Denver, 80202
303-844-2607

CONNECTICUT
330 Main Street, Second Floor
Hartford, 06106
203-240-4670

DELAWARE
844 King Street, Room 5207
Wilmington, 19801
302-573-6295

DISTRICT OF COLUMBIA
Small Business Administration
  (Main Office)
1441 L Street, NW
Washington, DC 20416

111 Eighteenth Street, NW,
  Sixth Floor
Washington, DC 20036
202-634-4950

FLORIDA
1320 South Dixie Highway,
  Suite 501
Coral Gables, 33136
305-536-5533

400 West Bay Street, Room 261
Jacksonville, 32202
904-791-3782

700 Twiggs Street, Room 607
Tampa, 33602
813-228-2594

3500 Forty-Fifth Street, Suite 6
West Palm Beach, 33407
305-689-2223

GEORGIA
1375 Peachtree Street, NE,
  Fifth Floor
Atlanta, 30367
404-347-4999

HAWAII
300 Ala Moana, Room 2213
Honolulu, 96850
808-541-2990

IDAHO
1020 Main Street, Second Floor
Boise, 83702
208-334-1696

ILLINOIS
219 South Dearborn Street,
  Room 437
Chicago, 60604
312-353-4528

Four North Old State Capitol
  Plaza
Springfield, 62701

INDIANA
575 North Penna Street,
  Room 578
Indianapolis, 46204
317-269-7272

IOWA
373 Collins Road, NE,
  Room 100
Cedar Rapids, 52402
319-399-2571

210 Walnut Street, Room 749
Des Moines, 50309

KANSAS
110 East Waterman Street
Wichita, 67202
316-269-6571

KENTUCKY
600 Federal Place, Room 188
Louisville, 40202

LOUISIANA
1661 Canal Street, Suite 2000
New Orleans, 70112
504-589-6685

500 Fannin Street, Room 8A08
Shreveport, 71101
318-226-5196

MAINE
40 Western Avenue, Room 512
Augusta, 04330
207-622-8378

MARYLAND
10 North Calvert Street
Baltimore, 21202

MASSACHUSETTS
10 Causeway Street,
  Room 265
Boston, 02222
617-565-5561

MICHIGAN
477 Michigan Avenue,
  Room 515
Detroit, 48226
313-266-6075

300 South Front Street
Marquette, 49885
906-225-1108

MINNESOTA
100 North Sixth Street,
  Suite 610
Minneapolis, 55403
612-349-3530

MISSOURI
1103 Grand Avenue,
  Sixth Floor
Kansas City, 64106
818-374-3416

815 Olive Street,
  Room 242
St. Louis, 63101
314-425-6600

MONTANA
301 South Park Avenue,
  Room 528
Helena, 59626
406-449-5381

NEBRASKA
11145 Mill Valley Road
Omaha, 68154
402-221-4691

NEVADA
301 East Stewart
Las Vegas, 89125
702-885-4602

50 South Virginia Street,
    Room 238
Reno, 89505
702-784-5268

NEW HAMPSHIRE
55 Pleasant Street, Room 210
Concord, 03301
603-225-4400

NEW JERSEY
2600 Mt. Ephrain
Camden, 08104
609-757-5183

60 Park Place, Fourth Floor
Newark, 07102
201-645-3580

NEW MEXICO
500 Marble Avenue, NE, Patio
    Plaza Building, Room 320
Albuquerque, 87100
505-262-6171

NEW YORK
445 Broadway, Room 242
Albany, 12207
518-472-6300

111 West Huron Street, Room
    1311
Buffalo, 14202
716-846-4301

333 East Water Street,
    Fourth Floor
Elmira, 14901
607-734-6610

35 Pinelawn Road, Room 102E
Melville, 11747
516-454-0764

26 Federal Plaza, Room 3100
New York, 10278
212-264-1318

100 State Street, Room 601
Rochester, 14614
716-263-6700

100 South Clinton Street,
    Room 1071
Syracuse, 13260
315-423-5371

NORTH CAROLINA
222 South Church Street,
    Room 300
Charlotte, 28202
704-371-6563

NORTH DAKOTA
657 Second Avenue North,
    Room 218
Fargo, 58102
701-237-5771

OHIO
550 Main Street, Room 5028
Cincinnati, 45202
513-684-2814

1240 East Ninth Street,
    Room 317
Cleveland, 44199
216-522-4182

85 Marconi Boulevard,
    Room 512
Columbus, 43215
614-469-6860

OKLAHOMA
200 NW Fifth Street, Suite 670
Oklahoma City, 73102
405-231-4301

OREGON
1220 SW Third Avenue,
Room 676
Portland, 97204
503-423-5221

PENNSYLVANIA
100 Chestnut Street, Suite 309
Harrisburg, 17101
717-782-3840

231 St. Asaphs Road,
Suite 400 East
Philadelphia, 19004
215-596-5801

960 Penn Street, Fifth Floor
Pittsburgh, 15222
412-644-4306

20 North Pennsylvania
Avenue, Room 2327
Wilkes-Barre, 18701
717-826-6497

PUERTO RICO
Carlos Chardon Avenue,
Federico Degatan
Federal Building, Room 691
Hato Rey, 00918
809-753-4003

RHODE ISLAND
380 Westminster Mall,
Fifth Floor
Providence, 02903
401-528-4586

SOUTH CAROLINA
1835 Assembly Street,
Third Floor
Columbia, 29202
803-765-5339

SOUTH DAKOTA
101 South Main Street,
Suite 101
Sioux Falls, 57102
605-336-2980

TENNESSEE
404 James Robertson Parkway,
Suite 1012
Nashville, 37219
615-736-5881

TEXAS
400 Mann Street, Suite 403
Corpus Christi, 78401
512-888-3331

1100 Commerce Street,
Room 3C36
Dallas, 75242
214-767-0608

10737 Gateway West, Suite 320
El Paso, 79935
915-541-7676

819 Taylor Street
Fort Worth, 76102
817-334-3777

222 East Van Buren Street,
Room 500
Harlingen, 78550
512-427-8533

2525 Murworth, Room 112
Houston, 77054
713-660-4407

TEXAS *(Continued)*
1611 Tenth Street, Suite 200
Lubbock, 79401
806-743-7462

505 East Travis, Room 103
Marshall, 75670
903-935-5257

727 East Durango Street,
   Room A-513
San Antonio, 78206
512-229-6105

UTAH
125 South State Street,
   Room 2237
Salt Lake City, 84138
801-524-5804

VERMONT
87 State Street, Room 205
Montpelier, 05602
802-828-4474

VIRGIN ISLANDS
Veterans Drive, Room 210
St. Thomas, 00801
809-774-8530

VIRGINIA
400 North Eighth Street,
   Room 3015
Richmond, 23240
804-771-2741

WASHINGTON
915 Second Avenue, Room
   3015
Seattle, 98174
206-442-5534

W920 Riverside Avenue,
   Room 651
Spokane, 99210
519-456-3781

WEST VIRGINIA
550 Eagan Street, Room 309
Charleston, 25301
304-347-5220

168 West Main Street,
   Fifth Floor
Clarksburg, 26301
304-623-5631

WISCONSIN
500 South Barstow Street,
   Room 37
Eau Claire, 54701
715-834-9012

212 East Washington Avenue,
   Room 213
Madison, 53703
608-264-5268

310 West Wisconsin Avenue,
   Room 400
Milwaukee, 53203
414-291-3941

WYOMING
100 East B Street, Room 4001
Casper, 82602
307-261-5761

TRADE SHOWS

Virtually every industry has one or two trade shows every year. I can't stress enough how important these events are for formulating ideas and making contacts. People who simply refuse to take your phone calls are happy to chat with you, person to person, for as long as you like. And next time, they will take your call. If you can possibly attend the shows that interest you, I'm sure you'll find them worthwhile.

For every show I've ever attended, the price of admission is a business card. If you have some printed that include your address and telephone number, with ". . . and Associates" after your name, and "New Product Development" underneath, it'll get you admittance to any show you care to see. In the United States, you're whatever your business card says you are. If you don't want to have cards printed, most shows will sell you a guest pass for $10 to $25.

The following list of shows is far from exhaustive; it merely indicates the breadth of these events. For a comprehensive list of shows, dates, and venues, ask your librarian to show you the *Directory of Conventions*, published by *Successful Meetings*, 633 Third Avenue, New York, NY 10017.

Consumer Electronics Show	202-457-4919
National China, Glass and Collectibles Show	212-686-6070
Transworld Housewares and Variety Show	312-442-8434
International Gift Show	212-686-6070
National Back-To-School Show	516-627-4000
American International Toy Fair	212-675-1141
Variety Merchandise Show	516-627-4000
San Francisco Food and Beverage Show	212-686-6070
Premium Incentive Show	516-627-4000
International Contemporary Furniture Show	212-686-6070
National Stationery Show	212-686-6070
Hotel and Motel Show	212-686-6070

National Hardware Show	203-964-0000
Action Sports Expo	714-499-5375
Bed, Bath and Linen Show	212-689-5550
National Shoe Fair	516-674-0200
Kids Fashion Show	212-594-0880
Surf Expo	404-220-2440

ANNUAL LICENSING SHOW

Every June, the *Annual Licensing and Merchandising Conference and Exposition* takes place at the New York Hilton Hotel. Everyone calls it simply, the Licensing Show. This is where people gather to exhibit and license their newly created cartoons, graphics, and creatures (real and mythical) to T-shirt companies, lunch box manufacturers, and cereal producers. If you've created the next Teenage Mutant Ninja Turtles, you'll probably want to learn more about this event.

Sponsor:

International Licensing Industry
Merchandisers Association
350 Fifth Avenue, Suite 6210
New York, NY 10118
212-244-1944

Show Producer:

Expocon Management
    Associates, Inc.
Seven Cambridge Drive
P.O. Box 1019
Trumbull, CT 06611
203-374-1411

FORM VA
UNITED STATES COPYRIGHT OFFICE

REGISTRATION NUMBER

_____

VA _____ VAU
EFFECTIVE DATE OF REGISTRATION

_____

Month   Day   Year

DO NOT WRITE ABOVE THIS LINE. IF YOU NEED MORE SPACE, USE A SEPARATE CONTINUATION SHEET.

1

TITLE OF THIS WORK ▼

NATURE OF THIS WORK ▼ See instructions

PREVIOUS OR ALTERNATIVE TITLES ▼

PUBLICATION AS A CONTRIBUTION If this work was published as a contribution to a periodical, serial, or collection, give information about the collective work in which the contribution appeared.   **Title of Collective Work ▼**

If published in a periodical or serial give: **Volume ▼**   **Number ▼**   **Issue Date ▼**   **On Pages ▼**

2

a

NAME OF AUTHOR ▼

DATES OF BIRTH AND DEATH
Year Born ▼   Year Died ▼

Was this contribution to the work a "work made for hire"?
☐ Yes
☐ No

AUTHOR'S NATIONALITY OR DOMICILE
Name of Country
OR { Citizen of ▶ _____
Domiciled in ▶ _____

WAS THIS AUTHOR'S CONTRIBUTION TO THE WORK
Anonymous?   ☐ Yes ☐ No
Pseudonymous?   ☐ Yes ☐ No
If the answer to either of these questions is "Yes," see detailed instructions

NATURE OF AUTHORSHIP Briefly describe nature of the material created by this author in which copyright is claimed. ▼

NOTE

Under the law the "author" of a work made for hire" is generally the employer not the employee (see instructions) For any part of this work that was "made for hire" check "Yes" in the space provided give the employer (or other person for whom the work was prepared) as "Author" of that part, and leave the space for dates of birth and death blank

b

NAME OF AUTHOR ▼

DATES OF BIRTH AND DEATH
Year Born ▼   Year Died ▼

Was this contribution to the work a "work made for hire"?
☐ Yes
☐ No

AUTHOR'S NATIONALITY OR DOMICILE
Name of country
OR { Citizen of ▶ _____
Domiciled in ▶ _____

WAS THIS AUTHOR'S CONTRIBUTION TO THE WORK
Anonymous?   ☐ Yes ☐ No
Pseudonymous?   ☐ Yes ☐ No
If the answer to either of these questions is "Yes" see detailed instructions

NATURE OF AUTHORSHIP Briefly describe nature of the material created by this author in which copyright is claimed. ▼

c

NAME OF AUTHOR ▼

DATES OF BIRTH AND DEATH
Year Born ▼   Year Died ▼

Was this contribution to the work a "work made for hire"?
☐ Yes
☐ No

AUTHOR'S NATIONALITY OR DOMICILE
Name of country
OR { Citizen of ▶ _____
Domiciled in ▶ _____

WAS THIS AUTHOR'S CONTRIBUTION TO THE WORK
Anonymous?   ☐ Yes ☐ No
Pseudonymous?   ☐ Yes ☐ No
If the answer to either of these questions is "Yes" see detailed instructions

NATURE OF AUTHORSHIP Briefly describe nature of the material created by this author in which copyright is claimed. ▼

3

a

YEAR IN WHICH CREATION OF THIS WORK WAS COMPLETED This information must be given ◀ Year in all cases.

b

DATE AND NATION OF FIRST PUBLICATION OF THIS PARTICULAR WORK
Complete this information Month ▶ _____ Day ▶ _____ Year ▶ _____ ◀ Nation
ONLY if this work has been published.

4

COPYRIGHT CLAIMANT(S) Name and address must be given even if the claimant is the same as the author given in space 2.▼

See instructions before completing this space

DO NOT WRITE HERE OFFICE USE ONLY

APPLICATION RECEIVED

ONE DEPOSIT RECEIVED

TWO DEPOSITS RECEIVED

REMITTANCE NUMBER AND DATE

TRANSFER If the claimant(s) named here in space 4 are different from the author(s) named in space 2, give a brief statement of how the claimant(s) obtained ownership of the copyright.▼

MORE ON BACK ▶
• Complete all applicable spaces (numbers 5-9) on the reverse side of this page
• See detailed instructions
• Sign the form at line 8

DO NOT WRITE HERE

Page 1 of _____ pages

EXAMINED BY		FORM VA
CHECKED BY		
☐ CORRESPONDENCE Yes		FOR COPYRIGHT OFFICE USE ONLY

DO NOT WRITE ABOVE THIS LINE. IF YOU NEED MORE SPACE, USE A SEPARATE CONTINUATION SHEET.

PREVIOUS REGISTRATION Has registration for this work, or for an earlier version of this work, already been made in the Copyright Office?

☐ Yes ☐ No If your answer is "Yes," why is another registration being sought? (Check appropriate box) ▼

☐ This is the first published edition of a work previously registered in unpublished form.

☐ This is the first application submitted by this author as copyright claimant.

☐ This is a changed version of the work, as shown by space 6 on this application.

If your answer is "Yes," give: **Previous Registration Number** ▼   **Year of Registration** ▼

5

DERIVATIVE WORK OR COMPILATION Complete both space 6a & 6b for a derivative work; complete only 6b for a compilation.

a. **Preexisting Material** Identify any preexisting work or works that this work is based on or incorporates. ▼

b. **Material Added to This Work** Give a brief, general statement of the material that has been added to this work and in which copyright is claimed. ▼

6

See instructions before completing this space

DEPOSIT ACCOUNT If the registration fee is to be charged to a Deposit Account established in the Copyright Office, give name and number of Account.

Name ▼   **Account Number** ▼

7

CORRESPONDENCE Give name and address to which correspondence about this application should be sent.   Name/Address/Apt/City/State/Zip ▼

Area Code & Telephone Number ▶

Be sure to give your daytime phone ◀ number

CERTIFICATION* I, the undersigned, hereby certify that I am the

Check only one ▼

☐ author

☐ other copyright claimant

☐ owner of exclusive right(s)

☐ authorized agent of _____

Name of author or other copyright claimant, or owner of exclusive right(s) ▲

8

of the work identified in this application and that the statements made by me in this application are correct to the best of my knowledge.

Typed or printed name and date ▼ If this application gives a date of publication in space 3, do not sign and submit it before that date.

_____ date ▶

Handwritten signature (X) ▼

MAIL CERTIFICATE TO	Name ▼	YOU MUST: • Complete all necessary spaces • Sign your application in space 8
		SEND ALL 3 ELEMENTS IN THE SAME PACKAGE:
Certificate will be mailed in window envelope	Number/Street/Apartment Number ▼	1. Application form 2. Non-refundable $10 filing fee in check or money order payable to Register of Copyrights 3. Deposit material
	City/State/ZIP ▼	MAIL TO: Register of Copyrights Library of Congress Washington, D.C. 20559

9

* 17 U.S.C. § 506(e) Any person who knowingly makes a false representation of a material fact in the application for copyright registration provided for by section 409, or in any written statement filed in connection with the application, shall be fined not more than $2,500.

June 1990—45,000   U.S. GOVERNMENT PRINTING OFFICE: 1990- 262-308:17

FORM TX
UNITED STATES COPYRIGHT OFFICE

REGISTRATION NUMBER

TX		TXU

EFFECTIVE DATE OF REGISTRATION

Month	Day	Year

DO NOT WRITE ABOVE THIS LINE. IF YOU NEED MORE SPACE, USE A SEPARATE CONTINUATION SHEET.

1

TITLE OF THIS WORK ▼

PREVIOUS OR ALTERNATIVE TITLES ▼

PUBLICATION AS A CONTRIBUTION If this work was published as a contribution to a periodical, serial, or collection, give information about the collective work in which the contribution appeared. **Title of Collective Work ▼**

If published in a periodical or serial give: **Volume ▼**   **Number ▼**   **Issue Date ▼**   **On Pages ▼**

2

a

NAME OF AUTHOR ▼

DATES OF BIRTH AND DEATH
Year Born ▼   Year Died ▼

Was this contribution to the work a "work made for hire"?
☐ Yes
☐ No

AUTHOR'S NATIONALITY OR DOMICILE
Name of Country
OR { Citizen of ▶ _____
{ Domiciled in ▶ _____

WAS THIS AUTHOR'S CONTRIBUTION TO THE WORK
Anonymous? ☐ Yes ☐ No
Pseudonymous? ☐ Yes ☐ No
If the answer to either of these questions is "Yes," see detailed instructions

NATURE OF AUTHORSHIP Briefly describe nature of the material created by this author in which copyright is claimed. ▼

NOTE

Under the law, the "author" of a work made for hire" is generally the employer, not the employee (see instructions). For any part of this work that was "made for hire" check "Yes" in the space provided, give the employer (or other person for whom the work was prepared) as "Author" of that part and leave the space for dates of birth and death blank.

b

NAME OF AUTHOR ▼

DATES OF BIRTH AND DEATH
Year Born ▼   Year Died ▼

Was this contribution to the work a "work made for hire"?
☐ Yes
☐ No

AUTHOR'S NATIONALITY OR DOMICILE
Name of country
OR { Citizen of ▶ _____
{ Domiciled in ▶ _____

WAS THIS AUTHOR'S CONTRIBUTION TO THE WORK
Anonymous? ☐ Yes ☐ No
Pseudonymous? ☐ Yes ☐ No
If the answer to either of these questions is "Yes," see detailed instructions

NATURE OF AUTHORSHIP Briefly describe nature of the material created by this author in which copyright is claimed. ▼

c

NAME OF AUTHOR ▼

DATES OF BIRTH AND DEATH
Year Born ▼   Year Died ▼

Was this contribution to the work a "work made for hire"?
☐ Yes
☐ No

AUTHOR'S NATIONALITY OR DOMICILE
Name of Country
OR { Citizen of ▶ _____
{ Domiciled in ▶ _____

WAS THIS AUTHOR'S CONTRIBUTION TO THE WORK
Anonymous? ☐ Yes ☐ No
Pseudonymous? ☐ Yes ☐ No
If the answer to either of these questions is "Yes," see detailed instructions

NATURE OF AUTHORSHIP Briefly describe nature of the material created by this author in which copyright is claimed. ▼

3

a

YEAR IN WHICH CREATION OF THIS WORK WAS COMPLETED This information must be given in all cases.
◄ Year

b

DATE AND NATION OF FIRST PUBLICATION OF THIS PARTICULAR WORK
Complete this information ONLY if this work has been published.
Month ▶ _____ Day ▶ _____ Year ▶ _____
◄ Nation

4

See instructions before completing this space

COPYRIGHT CLAIMANT(S) Name and address must be given even if the claimant is the same as the author given in space 2.▼

TRANSFER If the claimant(s) named here in space 4 are different from the author(s) named in space 2, give a brief statement of how the claimant(s) obtained ownership of the copyright.▼

APPLICATION RECEIVED

ONE DEPOSIT RECEIVED

TWO DEPOSITS RECEIVED

REMITTANCE NUMBER AND DATE

MORE ON BACK ▶ • Complete all applicable spaces (numbers 5-11) on the reverse side of this page.
• See detailed instructions.   • Sign the form at line 10.

DO NOT WRITE HERE
Page 1 of _____ pages

	FORM TX
EXAMINED BY	
CHECKED BY	
☐ CORRESPONDENCE Yes	FOR COPYRIGHT OFFICE USE ONLY

DO NOT WRITE ABOVE THIS LINE. IF YOU NEED MORE SPACE, USE A SEPARATE CONTINUATION SHEET.

PREVIOUS REGISTRATION Has registration for this work, or for an earlier version of this work, already been made in the Copyright Office?

☐ Yes ☐ No If your answer is "Yes," why is another registration being sought? (Check appropriate box) ▼

☐ This is the first published edition of a work previously registered in unpublished form.

☐ This is the first application submitted by this author as copyright claimant.

☐ This is a changed version of the work, as shown by space 6 on this application.

If your answer is "Yes," give: **Previous Registration Number ▼**   **Year of Registration ▼**

5

DERIVATIVE WORK OR COMPILATION Complete both space 6a & 6b for a derivative work; complete only 6b for a compilation.

a. **Preexisting Material** Identify any preexisting work or works that this work is based on or incorporates. ▼

b. **Material Added to This Work** Give a brief, general statement of the material that has been added to this work and in which copyright is claimed. ▼

See instructions before completing this space.

6

—space deleted—

7

REPRODUCTION FOR USE OF BLIND OR PHYSICALLY HANDICAPPED INDIVIDUALS A signature on this form at space 10, and a check in one of the boxes here in space 8, constitutes a non-exclusive grant of permission to the Library of Congress to reproduce and distribute solely for the blind and physically handicapped and under the conditions and limitations prescribed by the regulations of the Copyright Office: (1) copies of the work identified in space 1 of this application in Braille (or similar tactile symbols); or (2) phonorecords embodying a fixation of a reading of that work; or (3) both.

a ☐ Copies and Phonorecords   b ☐ Copies Only   c ☐ Phonorecords Only

See instructions

8

DEPOSIT ACCOUNT If the registration fee is to be charged to a Deposit Account established in the Copyright Office, give name and number of Account.

Name ▼   **Account Number ▼**

9

CORRESPONDENCE Give name and address to which correspondence about this application should be sent. Name/Address/Apt/City/State/Zip ▼

Area Code & Telephone Number ▶

Be sure to give your daytime phone ◀ number

CERTIFICATION* I, the undersigned, hereby certify that I am the

Check one ▶

☐ author

☐ other copyright claimant

☐ owner of exclusive right(s)

☐ authorized agent of

of the work identified in this application and that the statements made by me in this application are correct to the best of my knowledge.

Name of author or other copyright claimant, or owner of exclusive right(s) ▲

Typed or printed name and date ▼ If this application gives a date of publication in space 3, do not sign and submit it before that date.

date ▶

Handwritten signature (X) ▼

10

MAIL CERTIFI-CATE TO

Certificate will be mailed in window envelope

Name ▼

Number/Street/Apartment Number ▼

City/State/ZIP ▼

YOU MUST
• Complete all necessary spaces
• Sign your application in space 10
SEND ALL 3 ELEMENTS IN THE SAME PACKAGE
1. Application form
2. Non-refundable $10 filing fee in check or money order payable to Register of Copyrights
3. Deposit material
MAIL TO
Register of Copyrights
Library of Congress
Washington, D.C. 20559

11

* 17 U.S.C. § 506(e): Any person who knowingly makes a false representation of a material fact in the application for copyright registration provided for by section 409, or in any written statement filed in connection with the application, shall be fined not more than $2,500.

August 1989—300,000

U.S. GOVERNMENT PRINTING OFFICE: 1989-241-428 00.004

OMB No. 0651-0011 (12/31/86)

Applicant or Patentee: _____ Attorney's
Serial or Patent No.: _____ Docket No.: _____
Filed or Issued: _____
For: _____

VERIFIED STATEMENT (DECLARATION) CLAIMING SMALL ENTITY
STATUS (37 CFR 1.9 (f) and 1.27 (b)) — INDEPENDENT INVENTOR

As a below named inventor, I hereby declare that I qualify as an independent inventor as defined in 37 CFR 1.9 (c) for purposes of paying reduced fees under section 41 (a) and (b) of Title 35, United States Code, to the Patent and Trademark Office with regard to the invention entitled _____
described in

    [ ] the specification filed herewith
    [ ] application serial no. _____ , filed _____ .
    [ ] patent no. _____ , issued _____ .

I have not assigned, granted, conveyed or licensed and am under no obligation under contract or law to assign, grant, convey or license, any rights in the invention to any person who could not be classified as an independent inventor under 37 CFR 1.9 (c) if that person had made the invention, or to any concern which would not qualify as a small business concern under 37 CFR 1.9 (d) or a nonprofit organization under 37 CFR 1.9 (e).

Each person, concern or organization to which I have assigned, granted, conveyed, or licensed or am under an obligation under contract or law to assign, grant, convey, or license any rights in the invention is listed below:

    [ ] no such person, concern, or organization
    [ ] persons, concerns or organizations listed below*

    *NOTE: Separate verified statements are required from each named person, concern or organization having rights to the invention averring to their status as small entities. (37 CFR 1.27)

FULL NAME _____
ADDRESS _____
    [ ] INDIVIDUAL   [ ] SMALL BUSINESS CONCERN   [ ] NONPROFIT ORGANIZATION

FULL NAME _____
ADDRESS _____
    [ ] INDIVIDUAL   [ ] SMALL BUSINESS CONCERN   [ ] NONPROFIT ORGANIZATION

FULL NAME _____
ADDRESS _____
    [ ] INDIVIDUAL   [ ] SMALL BUSINESS CONCERN   [ ] NONPROFIT ORGANIZATION

I acknowledge the duty to file, in this application or patent, notification of any change in status resulting in loss of entitlement to small entity status prior to paying, or at the time of paying, the earliest of the issue fee or any maintenance fee due after the date on which status as a small entity is no longer appropriate. (37 CFR 1.28 (b))

I hereby declare that all statements made herein of my own knowledge are true and that all statements made on information and belief are believed to be true; and further that these statements were made with the knowledge that willful false statements and the like so made are punishable by fine or imprisonment, or both, under section 1001 of Title 18 of the United States Code, and that such willful false statements may jeopardize the validity of the application, any patent issuing thereon, or any patent to which this verified statement is directed.

_____   _____   _____
NAME OF INVENTOR   NAME OF INVENTOR   NAME OF INVENTOR

_____   _____   _____
Signature of Inventor   Signature of Inventor   Signature of Inventor

_____   _____   _____
Date   Date   Date

Form PTO-FB-A410 (8-83)

DECLARATION FOR PATENT APPLICATION

Docket Number (Optional)

As a below named inventor, I hereby declare that:

My residence, post office address and citizenship are as stated below next to my name.

I believe I am the original, first and sole inventor (if only one name is listed below) or an original, first and joint inventor (if plural names are listed below) of the subject matter which is claimed and for which a patent is sought on the invention entitled _____ , the specification of which

is attached hereto unless the following box is checked:

☐ was filed on _____ as United States Application Number or PCT International Application Number _____ and was amended on _____ (if applicable).

I hereby state that I have reviewed and understand the contents of the above identified specification, including the claims, as amended by any amendment referred to above.
I acknowledge the duty to disclose information which is material to patentability as defined in Title 37, Code of Federal Regulations, § 1.56.
I hereby claim foreign priority benefits under Title 35, United States Code, § 119 of any foreign application(s) for patent or inventor's certificate listed below and have also identified below any foreign application for patent or inventor's certificate having a filing date before that of the application on which priority is claimed.

Prior Foreign Application(s)

(Number)	(Country)	(Day/Month/Year Filed)
(Number)	(Country)	(Day/Month/Year Filed)
(Number)	(Country)	(Day/Month/Year Filed)

Priority Claimed
☐ Yes ☐ No
☐ Yes ☐ No
☐ Yes ☐ No

I hereby claim the benefit under Title 35, United States Code, § 120 of any United States application(s) listed below and, insofar as the subject matter of each of the claims of this application is not disclosed in the prior United States application in the manner provided by the first paragraph of Title 35, United States Code, § 112, I acknowledge the duty to disclose information which is material to patentability as defined in Title 37, Code of Federal Regulations, § 1.56 which became available between the filing date of the prior application and the national or PCT international filing date of this application.

(Application Number)	(Filing Date)	(Status – patented, pending, abandoned)
(Application Number)	(Filing Date)	(Status – patented, pending, abandoned)

I hereby appoint the following attorney(s) and/or agent(s) to prosecute this application and to transact all business in the Patent and Trademark Office connected therewith:

Address all telephone calls to _____ at telephone number _____
Address all correspondence to _____
_____
_____

I hereby declare that all statements made herein of my own knowledge are true and that all statements made on information and belief are believed to be true; and further that these statements were made with the knowledge that willful false statements and the like so made are punishable by fine or imprisonment, or both, under Section 1001 of Title 18 of the United States Code and that such willful false statements may jeopardize the validity of the application or any patent issued thereon.

Full name of sole or first inventor (given name, family name) _____
Inventor's signature _____ Date _____
Residence _____ Citizenship _____
Post Office Address _____

Full name of second joint inventor, if any (given name, family name) _____
Second Inventor's signature _____ Date _____
Residence _____ Citizenship _____
Post Office Address _____

☐ Additional inventors are being named on separately numbered sheets attached hereto.

Patent and Trademark Office; U.S. DEPARTMENT OF COMMERCE

PATENT APPLICATION TRANSMITTAL LETTER	Docket Number (Optional)

To the Commissioner of Patents and Trademarks:

Transmitted herewith for filing under 35 U.S.C. 111 and 37 CFR 1.53 is the patent application of

_____

entitled _____

_____

Enclosed are:

☐ _____ pages of written description, claims and abstract.

☐ _____ sheets of drawings.

☐ an assignment of the invention to _____

☐ executed declaration of the inventors.

☐ a certified copy of a _____ application.

☐ associate power of attorney.

☐ a verified statement to establish small entity status under 37 CFR 1.9 and 1.27.

☐ information disclosure statement

☐ preliminary amendment

☐ other: _____ .

CLAIMS AS FILED

	NUMBER FILED	NUMBER EXTRA	RATE	FEE
BASIC FEE			$690	$690
TOTAL CLAIMS	- 20 =	*	x $20	
INDEPENDENT CLAIMS	- 3 =	*	x $72	
MULTIPLE DEPENDENT CLAIM PRESENT			$220	

* NUMBER EXTRA MUST BE ZERO OR LARGER

		TOTAL	$
If applicant has small entity status under 37 CFR 1.9 and 1.27, then divide total fee by 2, and enter amount here.		SMALL ENTITY TOTAL	$

☐ A check in the amount of $ _____ to cover the filing fee is enclosed.

☐ The Commissioner is hereby authorized to charge and credit Deposit Account
No. _____ as described below. I have enclosed a duplicate copy of this sheet.

    ☐ Charge the amount of $ _____ as filing fee.

    ☐ Credit any overpayment.

    ☐ Charge any additional filing fees required under 37 CFR 1.16 and 1.17.

    ☐ Charge the issue fee set in 37 CFR 1.18 at the mailing of the Notice of
Allowance, pursuant to 37 CFR 1.311(b).

_____   _____

Date   Signature

    _____

           Typed or printed name

    _____

               Address

Patent and Trademark Office; U.S. DEPARTMENT OF COMMERCE

| AMENDMENT TO ALLEGE USE UNDER 37 CFR 2.76, WITH DECLARATION | MARK (Identify the mark) |
| | SERIAL NO |

TO THE ASSISTANT SECRETARY AND COMMISSIONER OF PATENTS AND TRADEMARKS:

APPLICANT NAME

Applicant requests registration of the above-identified trademark/service mark in the United States Patent and Trademark Office on the Principal Register established by the Act of July 5, 1946 (15 U.S.C. 1051 et. seq., as amended). Three specimens showing the mark as used in commerce are submitted with this amendment.

☐   Check here if Request to Divide under 37 CFR 2.87 is being submitted with this amendment.

Applicant is using the mark in commerce on or in connection with the following goods/services:

_____

_____

(NOTE: Goods/services listed above may not be broader than the goods/services identified in the application as filed)

Date of first use of mark anywhere: _____

Date of first use of mark in commerce
which the U.S. Congress may regulate: _____

Specify type of commerce: (e.g., interstate, between the U.S. and a specified foreign country) _____

Specify manner or mode of use of mark on or in connection with the goods/services: (e.g., trademark is applied to labels, service mark is used in advertisements) _____

The undersigned being hereby warned that willful false statements and the like so made are punishable by fine or imprisonment, or both, under 18 U.S.C. 1001, and that such willful false statements may jeopardize the validity of the application or any resulting registration, declares that he/she is properly authorized to execute this Amendment to Allege Use on behalf of the applicant; he/she believes the applicant to be the owner of the trademark/service mark sought to be registered; the trademark/ service mark is now in use in commerce; and all statements made of his/her own knowledge are true and all statements made on information and belief are believed to be true.

| Date | Signature |
| Telephone Number | Print or Type Name and Position |

U.S. DEPARTMENT OF COMMERCE/Patent and Trademark Office

AMENDMENT TRANSMITTAL LETTER		Docket Number (Optional)

Application Number	Filing Date	Examiner	Group Art Unit

Invention Title

TO THE COMMISSIONER OF PATENTS AND TRADEMARKS

Transmitted herewith is an amendment in the above - identified application.

☐ Small Entity status of this application has been established under 37 CFR 1.27 by a verified statement previously submitted.

☐ A verified statement to establish Small Entity status under 37 CFR 1.27 is enclosed.

☐ No additional fee is required.

☐ The fee has been calculated as shown below:

CLAIMS AS AMENDED

	(1) CLAIMS REMAINING AFTER AMENDMENT		(2) HIGHEST NUMBER PREVIOUSLY PAID FOR	(3) PRESENT NUMBER EXTRA	RATE	FEE
TOTAL CLAIMS	*	minus	**		x $20	
INDEPENDENT CLAIMS	*	minus	***		x $72	
MULTIPLE DEPENDENT CLAIM ADDED					$220	
					TOTAL	$
If applicant has small entity status under 37 CFR 1.9 and 1.27, then divide total fee by 2, and enter amount here.				SMALL ENTITY TOTAL		$

* If the entry in column 1 is less than the entry in column 2, write "0" in column 3
** If the highest number previously paid for IN THIS SPACE is less than 20, enter "20".
*** If the highest number previously paid for IN THIS SPACE is less than 3, enter "3".
The "highest number previously paid for" (total or independent) is the highest number found in the appropriate box in column 1.

☐ Please charge Deposit Account Number _____ in the amount of $ _____ .
A duplicate copy of this sheet is enclosed.

☐ A check in the amount of $ _____ to cover the filing fee is enclosed.

☐ The Commissioner is hereby authorized to charge payment of the following fees associated with this communication or credit any overpayment to Deposit Account Number _____ .
A duplicate copy of this sheet is enclosed.

☐ Any additional filing fees required under 37 CFR 1.16.

☐ Any patent application processing fees under 37 CFR 1.17.

Date	Signature

Patent and Trademark Office; U.S. DEPARTMENT OF COMMERCE

TRADEMARK/SERVICE MARK APPLICATION, PRINCIPAL REGISTER, WITH DECLARATION	MARK (Word(s) and/or Design)	CLASS NO. (If known)

TO THE ASSISTANT SECRETARY AND COMMISSIONER OF PATENTS AND TRADEMARKS:

APPLICANT'S NAME:

APPLICANT'S BUSINESS ADDRESS:
(Display address exactly as
it should appear on registration)

APPLICANT'S ENTITY TYPE: (**Check one** and supply requested information)

	Individual - Citizen of (Country):
	Partnership - State where organized (Country, if appropriate): _____ Names and Citizenship (Country) of General Partners: _____
	Corporation - State (Country, if appropriate) of Incorporation:
	Other (Specify Nature of Entity and Domicile):

GOODS AND/OR SERVICES:

Applicant requests registration of the trademark/service mark shown in the accompanying drawing in the United States Patent and Trademark Office on the Principal Register established by the Act of July 5, 1946 (15 U.S.C. 1051 et. seq., as amended) for the following goods/services (**SPECIFIC GOODS AND/OR SERVICES MUST BE INSERTED HERE**):

BASIS FOR APPLICATION: (Check boxes which apply, **but never both the first AND second boxes**, and supply requested information related to each box checked.)

[ ]	Applicant is using the mark in commerce on or in connection with the above identified goods/services. (15 U.S.C. 1051(a), as amended.) Three specimens showing the mark as used in commerce are submitted with this application. •Date of first use of the mark in commerce which the U.S. Congress may regulate (for example, interstate or between the U.S. and a foreign country): _____ •Specify the type of commerce: _____ (for example, interstate or between the U.S. and a specified foreign country) •Date of first use anywhere (the same as or before use in commerce date): _____ •Specify manner or mode of use of mark on or in connection with the goods/services: _____ (for example, trademark is applied to labels, service mark is used in advertisements)
[ ]	Applicant has a bona fide intention to use the mark in commerce on or in connection with the above identified goods/services. (15 U.S.C. 1051(b), as amended.) •Specify intended manner or mode of use of mark on or in connection with the goods/services: _____ (for example, trademark will be applied to labels, service mark will be used in advertisements)
[ ]	Applicant has a bona fide intention to use the mark in commerce on or in connection with the above identified goods/services, and asserts a claim of priority based upon a foreign application in accordance with 15 U.S.C. 1126(d), as amended. • Country of foreign filing: _____ • Date of foreign filing: _____
[ ]	Applicant has a bona fide intention to use the mark in commerce on or in connection with the above identified goods/services and, accompanying this application, submits a certification or certified copy of a foreign registration in accordance with 15 U.S.C. 1126(e), as amended. • Country of registration: _____ • Registration number: _____

NOTE: Declaration, on Reverse Side, MUST be Signed

PTO Form 1478 (REV. 5/91)
OMB No. 06510009 (Exp. 6/92)

U.S. DEPARTMENT OF COMMERCE/Patent and Trademark Office

DECLARATION

The undersigned being hereby warned that willful false statements and the like so made are punishable by fine or imprisonment, or both, under 18 U.S.C. 1001, and that such willful false statements may jeopardize the validity of the application or any resulting registration, declares that he/she is properly authorized to execute this application on behalf of the applicant; he/she believes the applicant to be the owner of the trademark/service mark sought to be registered, or, if the application is being filed under 15 U.S.C. 1051(b), he/she believes applicant to be entitled to use such mark in commerce; to the best of his/her knowledge and belief no other person, firm, corporation, or association has the right to use the above identified mark in commerce, either in the identical form thereof or in such near resemblance thereto as to be likely, when used on or in connection with the goods/services of such other person, to cause confusion, or to cause mistake, or to deceive; and that all statements made of his/her own knowledge are true and that all statements made on information and belief are believed to be true.

_____   _____
DATE   SIGNATURE

_____   _____
TELEPHONE NUMBER   PRINT OR TYPE NAME AND POSITION

INSTRUCTIONS AND INFORMATION FOR APPLICANT

TO RECEIVE A FILING DATE, THE APPLICATION <u>MUST</u> BE COMPLETED AND SIGNED BY THE APPLICANT AND SUBMITTED ALONG WITH:

1.　　The prescribed **FEE ($200.00)** for each class of goods/services listed in the application;
2.　　A **DRAWING PAGE** displaying the mark in conformance with 37 CFR 2.52;
3.　　If the application is based on use of the mark in commerce, **THREE (3) SPECIMENS** (evidence) of the mark as used in commerce for each class of goods/services listed in the application. All three specimens may be in the nature of: (a) labels showing the mark which are placed on the goods; (b) photographs of the mark as it appears on the goods, (c) brochures or advertisements showing the mark as used in connection with the services.
4.　　An **APPLICATION WITH DECLARATION** (this form) - The application must be signed in order for the application to receive a filing date. Only the following person may sign the declaration, depending on the applicant's legal entity: (a) the individual applicant; (b) an officer of the corporate applicant; (c) one general partner of a partnership applicant; (d) all joint applicants.

SEND APPLICATION FORM, DRAWING PAGE, FEE, AND SPECIMENS (IF APPROPRIATE) TO:

**U.S. DEPARTMENT OF COMMERCE
Patent and Trademark Office, Box TRADEMARK
Washington, D.C. 20231**

Additional information concerning the requirements for filing an application is available in a booklet entitled **Basic Facts About Trademarks**, which may be obtained by writing to the above address or by calling: (703) 305-HELP.

This form is estimated to take 15 minutes to complete. Time will vary depending upon the needs of the individual case. Any comments on the amount of time you require to complete this form should be sent to the Office of Management and Organization, U.S. Patent and Trademark Office, U.S. Department of Commerce, Washington D.C. 20231, and to the Office of Information and Regulatory Affairs, Office of Management and Budget, Washington, D.C. 20503.

INDEX